Microwave Cooking...
...made easy

Pra[illegible]

Publishers
UNICORN BOOKS
J-3/16, Daryaganj, New Delhi-110002
☎ 23276539, 23272783, 23272784 • *Fax:* 011-23260518
E-mail: unicornbooks@vsnl.com
Website: www.unicornbooks.in

Distributors
Pustak Mahal, Delhi
Bengaluru *e-mail*: pustak@airtelmail.in • pustak@sancharnet.in
Mumbai *e-mail*: rapidex@bom5.vsnl.net.in
Patna *e-mail*: rapidexptn@rediffmail.com
Hyderabad *e-mail*: pustakmahalhyd@yahoo.co.in

ISBN 978-81-7806-134-4

Edition : September 2009

Printed at : Param Offsetters, Okhla, New Delhi-110020

Introduction

'**Microwave Cooking ...made easy**' is about understanding a new method of cooking. As we all know, the use of microwave in the kitchen is nothing but using another source of energy for cooking. Microwave oven is a time saving device that is very helpful for housewives, working people, senior citizens, teenagers, and youngsters staying alone because of various reasons.

The microwave oven can be used for more tasks than just making tea/coffee or heating up leftovers. It can prove a blessing if used properly. Many a time, the first attempt makes or breaks a potential microwave enthusiast because most of us don't read the instruction manual/ cookbook properly, but just start operating this high-tech appliance. Therefore, a piece of advice for all beginners—go through the cookbook/manual before attempting any recipes as cooking timings are most important.

Microwave cooking helps in cutting down the time to almost half without any compromise in providing a variety of healthier meals to the family. The encouraging news is that the knowledge of conventional cooking of Grandma's recipes is not wasted, only the application of it is slightly different, and as said earlier, cooking timings are one of the most important factors involved here.

Once you learn how to effectively operate your microwave for different uses, it is a pleasure to work in the kitchen because a number of otherwise time-consuming dishes are cooked in a jiffy and your time thus saved is fruitfully utilised in other productive areas.

Acknowledgement

Special thanks to my dear husband Wg. Cdr. Mandhir Singh for his unrelenting support at each stage in the making of this book. I must thank my family, friends, well-wishers & the users of my previous books for their heartening rejoinders.

I would like to dedicate this book to my mother Mrs. Ripdaman Kalsi, my eternal *guru*.

Photographs are by Mr. Sanjay Jadav.

Contents

Soups and Salads 55

Starters and Evening Snacks 63

Main Course 81

INDIAN FLAVOURS 82

CONTINENTAL DELIGHTS 113

Some Facts about Microwave Oven and Its Working

There is so much mystery that surrounds microwave energy, but it is no different than any other energy used for cooking. Microwave cooking is done by radiation or electromagnetic waves given out by electricity. As soon as microwaves are converted to heat, they are absorbed by the food; about 4-inch wavelength penetrates ¾-2 inches into the surface of the food, but the air is not heated. Water molecules are very good absorbers of microwaves, sugar and fat are better, and salt is even better. That is why foods high in fat and sugar will cook relatively faster than foods made mainly of water. Salt water boils faster than normal/plain water and marinated pieces of meat and vegetables placed directly on the surface may overcook or develop dark patches if cooked for more than the specified time.

While cooking in a microwave oven a few things must be kept in mind:

a. Microwaves cook the food from the outside to the inside. If you watch carefully, you will notice that any dish starts boiling from the outer side first and then from the centre.

b. Stirring the dish from time to time redistributes heat from the outer layers to the inner layers.

c. Foods that cannot be stirred should be placed with the thicker pieces to the outside, e.g., chicken legs.

d. Foods that can't be arranged need to be shifted around to get an equal amount of heat. They are also turned over. Sometimes the hot liquid in the bottom of the dish transfers additional heat to the surface of the food kept on it and causes faster cooking.

e. The dishes that cannot be stirred or turned over are rotated sometimes, for example, cakes and pies, etc. If your oven cooks evenly, then ignore such instructions.

f. Dishes get hot due to heat conduction from the food, not from the microwave energy. Hot foods transfer heat to the sides of the dishes that they touch, not to the handles.

g. In microwave cooking, 'covers' retain heat and moisture, prevent food from dehydration and speed up cooking time. A tight glass lid or a plastic wrap, like cling film, will accomplish this. Cover the dish if the recipe demands it, or when you are reheating gravies, soups or stews, etc. Pizzas, burgers, patties or fried Indian snacks like samosa or pakoda, etc, should be loosely covered with paper napkins, its ends tucked under the dish while reheating. Leftover rice, dry vegetables, idlies or dhokla, etc., should be sprinkled with a few drops of water, covered with a lid and then reheated.

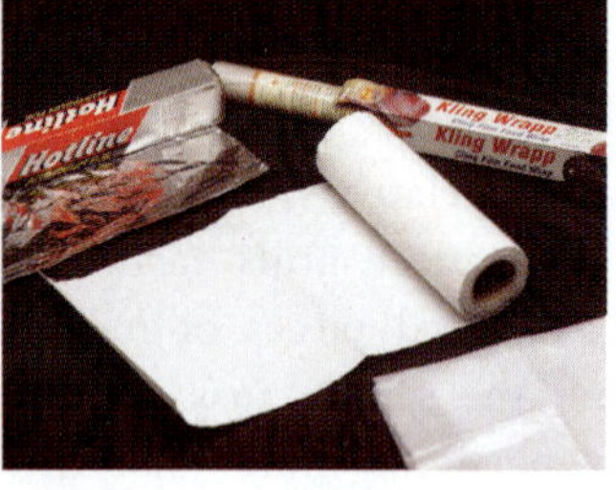

Note: The terminology of the recipe should be closely followed. For example:

Cover tightly: The dish to be cooked should be covered with a casserole lid or a plastic wrap that has been folded back at one corner to avoid splitting when steam builds up. If a dish requires more stirring, then a nice fitting lid should be used. **Do not cover food with aluminium foil while cooking in micro mode.**

Cook uncovered: It means that a drier cooked surface of the dish is desired, as sometimes liquid needs to be evaporated, e.g., from mushrooms, roasted meats, cakes and pastry crust, etc.

Important: Always open a tight lid or a cover away from you to prevent steam burns.

Cooking time: It is important to set the cooking or reheating timings carefully, otherwise foods can become hard and leathery, if overcooked. Under-cooked foods can still be cooked to satisfaction. If the volume in the recipe is increased or decreased, time adjustment is equally important.

Standing time: Food continues to be cooked for some time even after it is removed from the micro oven, therefore, it is essential to give it that standing time. Standing can be done in the oven or outside the oven on a kitchen platform but pastry crust, after being removed, should be kept on the wire rack so that moisture evaporates and pastry is crisp and not soggy. Even the cake baked in a micro oven looks very moist and undone but once it is kept outside, after about 10 minutes, it appears perfect.

In short, cooking in a microwave is a pleasure; though it is slightly tricky, but practice makes a man perfect. Therefore, do not hesitate, go ahead and enjoy cooking not only nutritive but also healthy food, as food prepared in a micro oven is cooked in its natural juices, which are sometimes lost in conventional cooking.

Types of Micro Ovens

These days many kinds of micro ovens are available in the market:

Microwave Model without Grill/Convection

This model is good for defrosting and thawing the food or reheating it directly from the refrigerator. Besides this, vegetables can be boiled, soups and stews can be made, fruits can be stewed, tea or coffee can be brewed, meats can be cooked, and pulaos and desserts can be prepared in this mode. Infants' milk bottles can be sterilised, their basic khichdi from dal-rice powder and other semi-solid foods can also be made. Despite all the above mentioned uses, **biscuits, cookies and short crust pastries can't be made, and toast also cannot be grilled**.

In Micro mode, China, heatproof glass dishes, pottery, specially designed plasticwares with their respective lids should be used for cooking and reheating. Paper bags, cloth kitchen towels, paper plates or wooden bowls can be used for reheating for a short duration. Plastic or cling film wraps can be used as covers for short duration. Wooden skewers and plastic/polythene bags can be used.

In Micro mode, China with gold and silver lines, delicate glass dishes, metal moulds, metal skewers and aluminium foil as cover or a wrap **should not** be used.

Microwave with Convection and Grill

This model has all the facilities of Microwave oven + Convection + Grill, but at one time one thing works.

Convection mode of a microwave oven becomes basically an electric oven used for baking and cooking, very much like an OTG (oven, toaster and griller).

In this mode microwave energy is not used, so all the utensils used in an ordinary electric oven or a cooking range can be used here. Heatproof glass dishes can also be used safely. Aluminium foil can be used as a cover.

Do not use paper plates or napkins, plastic cookwares, plastic bags, plastic lids or wraps as covers, and wooden skewers, etc.

In Convection mode, you can bake dishes, cakes, biscuits, cookies, pies and pizzas, etc. You can roast and bake fish/meat/chicken, etc.

In Grill mode, any heatproof dish or metal plate can be used as there are no microwaves at this moment. Toasts, open sandwiches, fish, chicken or cutlets can be grilled.

Combination of Micro+Oven and Micro+ Grill model

It helps you to do everything you want to cook or bake in a microwave oven. Simultaneously you can use combination of micro and oven or combination of Micro and Grill. You can grill separately and bake separately also.

Utensils used here must be heatproof and microwave safe only; e.g., glass dishes like Pyrex, Borosil and other micro-safe glass dishes and pottery.

Do not use metal moulds, China, wooden and metal skewers, aluminium foil, paper or cloth napkins, or even plastic wrap.

A variety of Continental dishes, puddings, cakes and meats can be cooked in this mode.

Right Utensils for Microwave Cooking

In Microwave mode, do not use utensils made of metal, i.e., steel, copper or brass, as microwaves could get reflected back to the magnetron tube and damage it.

- Metal cooking utensils slow down/stop microwave cooking completely, making it inefficient.
- Dishes with a metal trim, golden or silver lines should not be used as they can cause sparking, and the food will not be heated or cooked.
- **Always use dishes made of glass like Pyrex, Borosil** brand for reheating and cooking purposes. Other glass dishes marked as **Microwave Safe** can be used. Round and oval dishes are ideal. As the corners of square dishes absorb more microwave energy, the food at the corners tends to get over-cooked. In fact, the circle/doughnut shaped circle is the best for cooking food evenly.

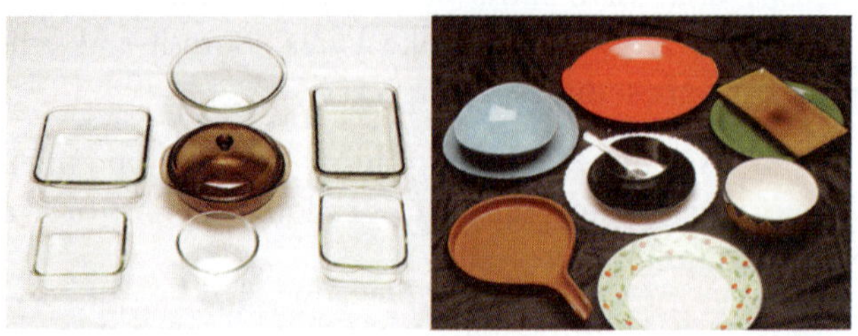

- **Ceramic crockery** (Bone China) without gold or silver lines and coloured **Pottery** (earthenwares like Khurja pottery) can be safely used.

- **Paper plates** without aluminium lining or **Wooden bowls** can be used for reheating dry snacks, but for a minute or two only.
- **Plastic cookwares especially designed for microwave ovens** can be used safely for both cooking and reheating. These have a hole at the top of the lid to release extra steam. Cooking pots, steaming baskets, cooking and storing containers are all easily available. Strong **Polythene bags** can be used for boiling potatoes, arvi or beetroot, etc.

  Do not cook for more than 10 minutes in plasticwares.

Care and Cleaning

1. The micro oven should not be operated without food or a glass of water in it.
2. Don't let the food accumulate around the door seals, else micro oven will not close properly.
3. Do not let the children mishandle the switches, controls and the buttons.
4. Keep your micro oven as clean as possible.
5. Disconnect from the electric supply and wipe it with damp cloth after use, or wipe the inside with a damp cloth soaked in mild soap/detergent and dry it clean with a soft cloth.
6. Do not use abrasive cleaner or scrubbing pad, it may cause scratches.
7. If any fishy smell lingers in and around microwave oven, place a bowl of water with 2 tbsp lemon juice in it and heat it to boiling point; leave it inside for a few minutes and remove. Wipe the inside with a soft cotton cloth.

Important Dos and Don'ts

- Always sprinkle a few drops of water over the leftover food and cover it with a lid or cling film before reheating it.
- Always preheat the oven before using the Convection mode.
- Always follow the cooking time mentioned in a recipe properly before trying it in a microwave mode.
- Always wrap chapaties/parathas in a moist towel/ napkin before reheating them.
- Always use deep dishes to prepare gravies and soups to avoid spillage.
- Always give standing time to a dish cooked in a micro oven before it is served, unless it is mentioned 'Serve immediately'.
- Always open the lid of a dish away from your body to avoid any steam burns.
- Always place dish on wire rack for baking in Convection mode or while grilling to get even heat.
- Prefer to cook in a round container in a micro oven, as foods in a rectangular or square dish tend to be overcooked at the corners. If you have to cook in these dishes, protect the corners from overcooking by placing small pieces of aluminium foil there.
- Always place a piece of aluminium foil over the glass surface before making tandoori tikkas/grilling the fish or preparing tikkies, etc.
- Always pierce the skin of potatoes and tomatoes before cooking if they are being cooked whole.
- Always keep your oven clean.

- Always remove the plastic wrapping of food before cooking.
- Always use dish pads or oven gloves to remove cooked/ heated food from the oven.
- Do not overcook food in Microwave mode because it tends to become leathery.
- Do not add more water than required while boiling/ cooking vegetables for salads or any other dry preparation. A little water prevents vegetables from drying out and vegetables cooked in their own juices retain all the vitamins and minerals, hence, healthier food.
- Do not deep fry in the microwave because the temperature of oil can't be controlled.
- Do not use aluminium foil for covering dishes in Microwave mode.
- Do not reheat Indian sweets with Silver Vark on them in microwave mode. For slight heating you may cover them with a lid or a plate.
- Do not cook eggs in their shells in Microwave mode, as the pressure will cause them to explode. Even while cooking a single fried egg, do not forget to pierce its yolk.
- Do not cover the ventilation slots of your microwave oven.
- Do not cook liquids or other food in sealed containers, they may explode.
- Do no let small children operate the micro oven on their own.
- Do not try to repair your micro oven yourself if it is not working properly.
- Do not operate the empty micro oven for trial, keep a glass of water in it.
- Do not operate microwave oven when the voltage is low or fluctuating constantly. It will not be effective at all.

Defrosting Chart

Food at room temperature cooks faster in comparison to frozen food, hence, it is important to thaw it. Defrosting in a microwave is quick. It is more hygienic and retains the natural colour, texture and flavour of the food.

Remove the food from its pouch or prick the bag to avoid bursting. Place in a circular pattern on the turntable and turn it half way through for even defrosting.

Food Item	*Weight*	*Defrosting Time*	*Standing Time*
Fish	500 gm	10 minutes	15 minutes
Chicken Pieces	800 gm	15 minutes	15 minutes
Chicken Whole	800 gm	20 to 25 minutes	25 to 30 minutes
Minced Meat	500 gm	5 to 6 minutes	15 minutes
Mutton	500 gm	10 minutes	15 minutes
Liver	500 gm	8 minutes	15 minutes
Lamb Chops	500 gm	5 to 6 minutes	10 minutes
Sausages	500 gm	5 to 6 minutes	10 minutes
Frozen Vegetables (chopped)	500 gm	5 minutes	8 to 10 minutes

Note: While writing the cooking timings, it is presumed that the ingredients used in any recipe are at room temperature.

Reheating Chart

Reheating food in the microwave is quick and without any loss of quality or texture. It tastes as though freshly cooked. Even individual servings can be reheated at a lower power setting.

Food Items	*Approximate weight/Portions*	*Reheating Time*
Baby food	100 ml	10 seconds in a glass bowl
Bread/Rolls	2	30 seconds in a paper plate
Sandwich	2	1 minute wrapped in a paper napkin
Pizza	1 whole	2 min. covered with cling film
Burger/Hotdog	1	1 min. wrapped in paper towel
Gulab Jamuns	6 to 8	40 sec. in a glass dish, covered
Burfi/Laddoo	4 to 6	30 sec. uncovered, wait and serve
Parathas/Chapaties	8 to 10	1 min. wrapped in a moist cloth
Porridge/Dalia	1 helping	1 minute in a glass bowl
Sauces	250 ml	2 min. in a glass bowl
Soup	1 helping	1½ minutes
Rice	250 gm	2 min. in a glass dish, covered
Dry vegetables	2 servings	2 minutes, covered
Vegetables in gravy	2 servings	3 minutes, covered
Chicken dry	2 servings	2 minutes, covered
Chicken curry	2 servings	3 minutes, covered
Meat curry	2 servings	3 minutes, covered
Fish fry	2 servings	2 minutes, uncovered
Fish curry	2 servings	3 minutes, covered
Idlis	4 no	30 seconds, covered
Dals	2 helpings	3 minutes, covered
Halwas	250 gm	2 minutes, covered

Dishes taken out of refrigerator should be spread on a plate and covered for effective and uniform heating.

Dish covers, cling wrap or wax paper can be used to cover. Dishes with gravy should be stirred in between to distribute the heat.

Add a little gravy, water or milk to the dry dishes before heating (according to the suitability of the dish).

Wrap breads in a paper towel or paper to absorb moisture. Do not use newspaper.

Test by feeling the bottom of the plate or a dish. If it feels hot, the food is properly reheated.

When reheating in a plate, place thick food towards outside and delicate food in the centre.

Determine the Wattage of your Microwave Oven

You can determine the wattage of a microwave by placing 1 cup of water in a 2-cup measuring cup. Heat on High for 2 minutes. If the water boils in two minutes or less, the microwave is probably 700 watts or more. If it takes longer then it is 600 watts or less.

Power Equivalents

High	=	100% power,
Medium	=	80% to 60%,
Low	=	40% to 20%.

Cooking something that takes an hour in the oven should take about 15 minutes in the microwave oven.

Useful and Interesting Microwave Tips

Here is a long list of tips to use your micro oven to its full capacity and make it indispensable.

Blanch Almonds

Fill half a small micro-safe bowl with water and place ¼ cup almonds. Microwave for 3 minutes on micro High. Stand for 2 minutes, remove, cool and peel.

Bread Cubes Dried

Place 3 to 4 cups fresh or stale bread cut into cubes on the turntable and heat on micro High for 4 to 5 minutes stirring once in between. Give some standing time and use Bread Croutons with soups and salads or pass through a mixer to make Breadcrumbs.

Blanch Tomatoes

Wash and place 4 to 6 tomatoes in a shallow dish; give a small cut on the stem side of each tomato and cook on micro High for 3 minutes. Cool, peel off the skin and use.

Boil Milk

Boil 1000 ml milk for 15 minutes on micro Medium.

Boiling Potatoes and Arvi

Peel, wash and place 5 to 6 medium sized potatoes in a strong polythene bag and cook on micro High for 8 minutes. Stand for 2 minutes, then use as required.

Wash ½ kg arvi and place in a plastic bag and micro cook for 10 minutes. Remove, cool, peel and use.

Chili Oil

Mix 1 cup cooking oil and ¼ cup deseeded and broken dry red chilies; cook on High for 7 minutes, uncovered; cool; leave overnight covered; strain thoroughly and collect oil. Store in a clean bottle and use as required.

Dry Mint leaves (pudina)

Wash and remove mint leaves from the stems. Take 2 cups of leaves and place them on a dry kitchen towel to soak any extra water. Place them on the turntable of micro oven and dry on micro High for 4 minutes, stirring once in between. Stand inside the oven for 10 minutes, remove and cool thoroughly before storing. Powder and use as and when required. In the same way dry Methi leaves (fenugreek) and Curry leaves, i.e. Curry patta.

Dry roast the Nuts

Place ½ cup peanuts/cashew nuts or almonds in a paper bag and roast on micro High for 3 minutes, shaking the bag once in between. For fried look, smear the nuts with a little oil or butter before placing them in the paper bag. Serve with a pinch of salt mixed later as a snack or use the nuts the way it is required in any recipe.

Dry fry Dalia (broken wheat) or Suji, i.e. Semolina

Place 250 gm dalia or suji in a paper bag and dry fry on micro High for 3 minutes, shaking the bag once in between. In this way dry the Dals/Flour also before storing if you are staying in a coastal area.

Freshen the soggy Wafers/Dry Snacks/Chewda/ Biscuits, etc

Place biscuits and wafers on paper napkins or on a plate, and cook uncovered on High for 1 minute, wait for a few minutes to cool down and get crisp. Similarly, any mixture/chewda or corn flakes, etc, can be placed in a shallow bowl and microwaved for 1 minute.

Jams and Honey Softened

Refrigerated jams and honey become soft enough to spread/pour without changing colour or texture if heated in a microwave. Open the jar lid and heat on micro High for 1½ to 2 minutes.

Jaggery (gur) Syrup

Soak 1 cup grated jaggery in 1 cup water for 10 minutes and then cook on micro High for 4 minutes. Cool, strain and store under refrigeration. It is ideal to be used in place of white sugar in tea or herbal beverages.

Making of Coffee

Boil together ½ cup milk and ½ cup water on Reheat mode of your microwave or boil on High for 2½ to 3 minutes and remove. Add ½ tsp coffee powder and 1 tsp sugar after a few seconds; stir and enjoy it.

Making of Desi Ghee or Clarified Butter.

Place 2 cups white butter or cream in a deep micro-safe bowl and heat on micro High for 3 minutes, covered. Stir it and cook on micro Low for 15 minutes, uncovered. Let it stand for 1 hour and then slowly strain it through a fine sieve, collect the ghee and store it.

Making of Paneer

Put 1000 ml milk in a deep micro-safe bowl and heat it on micro Medium for 15 minutes. Take it out, mix 2 tbsp lemon juice and boil on micro Low for another 10 minutes. Let it stand for 30 minutes to 1 hour; strain it through a fine sieve and let the solids stand in the sieve for 20 to 30 minutes. Collect the paneer and store under refrigeration. Don't throw the Whey but use it to make nourishing and healthy beverages.

Making of Tea

Boil 1 cup water on Reheating mode or on micro High for 2 to 3 minutes; add 1 tsp tea leaves or 1 tea bag in it; stand for 2 minutes for brewing and remove. Heat ¼ cup milk for 30 seconds and add; strain the tea or squeeze the tea bag and discard. Add sugar to taste.

Morning cup of Lemon-Honey

Non-tea drinkers can make a cup of lemon-honey first thing in the morning. Boil 1 cup water, squeeze ½ a lemon, add 1 tsp honey and enjoy the hot tea. Or add ½ tsp tea leaves into lemon water; leave for 2 minutes for brewing; add sugar and enjoy it.

Peels Dried

Cut lemon or orange peels into very thin strips. Take about 3 tbsp and spread them on a paper plate and heat on micro High for 3 minutes or until dry but not burnt. Watch the process closely and stir once in between. Cool and store under refrigeration.

Pop the Corn

In a big brown or white paper bag, place ½ cup popping corn and gently fold the mouth of the bag twice to close lightly. Cook on micro High for 3 minutes. Remove in a serving bowl and sprinkle a little salt, shake the bowl to mix salt properly and serve the popcorn hot.

Note: Always cook popcorn in small quantity. Do not try popcorns in the low wattage micro oven.

Preserve Pineapple

Clean and cut 1 pineapple into slices; boil together 1½ cups of sugar and 2 cups of water on High for 10 minutes; add pineapple slices and cook on High for 12 minutes. Cool and keep in the deep freezer. It can last for many months. Take out as much as you require at one time.

Roast Papad

Place 4 to 6 papad in a paper bag and roast them for 1½ to 2 minutes, changing side once. For getting the fried look of papad, brush them with oil and roast the same way. You may place 2 papad on a paper napkin and roast for 1 minute, changing side once in between.

Soften Dates and Raisins

Keep 1 cup dates or raisins, sprinkle 1 tbsp water over them. Cover and heat on micro High for 45 seconds. Let them stand for a minute or so covered and then serve after meals.

Softening hard Butter

Place butter in a micro-safe butter dish and heat on Defrost for 30 seconds.

Softening Ice cream

Place 1 slab of ice cream on a micro-safe plate in the oven and heat on Defrost for 30 seconds.

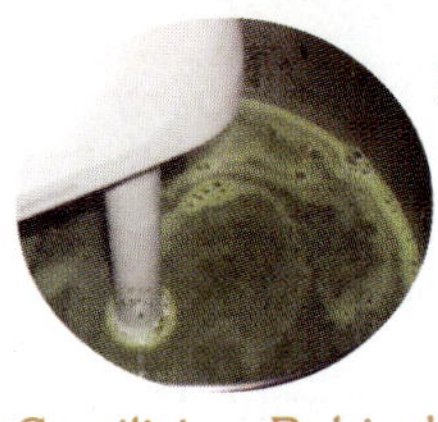

Spinach Puree

Cook 4 cups chopped Spinach for 5 minutes on micro High. Cool and puree it for different uses.

Sterilising Babies' Milk Bottles

Place the baby's bottles and accessories with 2 cups water in a big micro-safe bowl and boil for 6 to 7 minutes on High to sterilise.

Stewing of fresh Fruits

Place 1 cup cut fruits in a micro-safe bowl and cook on micro High for 3 to 4 minutes, covered.

Toasting Sesame seeds

Spread ½ cup sesame seeds on a paper plate or a paper napkin and heat on micro High for 2 to 3 minutes. Watch it closely and stir once in between.

Tomato Puree

Cook 5 cups of chopped tomatoes on micro High for 20 minutes. Stir in between to redistribute heat. Cool and puree. Use as required.

Warming up of Lemons, Oranges and Sweet Lime for yielding more juice

Warm up Lemons, Limes, Mosambies or Keenus for 30 to 40 seconds to yield more juice.

Warming up Babies' Milk

Warm up baby's milk for 30 seconds before feeding.

Basic Pastes, Sauces, Relishes

1. Basic Onion and Tomato Paste

Micro Cooking: 35 mins

- Onions ... *1000 gm*
- Tomatoes ... *1000 gm*
- Ginger-Garlic paste ... *3 tbsp*
- Cooking oil ... *5 tbsp*
- Cumin ... *2 tsp*
- Chili powder ... *2 tsp*
- Turmeric powder...*2 tsp*
- Salt ... *1 tbsp*

- Mixed Spice powder ... *1 tbsp*

Preparation and Cooking

1. Cut onions into thin slices, mix with 3 tbsp cooking oil and microwave on High for 10 minutes uncovered, stirring once in between. Sprinkle 1 tsp salt, stir and cook for 3 minutes more on High, uncovered.
2. Blanch tomatoes on micro High for 5 minutes; remove and cool; peel the skin; roughly chop them; mix with onions and make a fine paste. Or chop unblanched tomatoes and grind with cooked onions.
3. In a deep micro-safe bowl add 2 tbsp oil and cumin and microwave on High for 2 minutes.
4. In the same bowl add onion and tomato paste, ginger-garlic paste, turmeric and chili powders, salt and mixed spice powder (garam masala). Cover it with a lid and microwave on High for 15 minutes.

5. Let it stand for 5 minutes and open the lid. Your thick masala/paste is ready; cool, divide and store in small containers; mark and place in the deep freezer.
6. Take out as required half an hour before use.

Yield: This quantity will give you approximately 4 cups of thick masala.

While cooking with this paste, please keep in mind that some salt, spices and chili powder have already been added to it, so adjust the seasoning accordingly.

2. Chili-Garlic Sauce

Micro Cooking: 12 mins

- Dry Red Chilies ... *2 cups* (broken and deseeded)
- Garlic peeled ... *1 cup*
- Vinegar ... *1 cup*
- Salt ... *4 tsp*
- Oil ... *¼ cup*

Preparation and Cooking

1. Heat 2 cups water in a micro-safe bowl for 2 minutes.
2. Wash and soak red chilies in this water for 1 hour.
3. Cook them in the same water, covered, for 8 minutes on micro High. Let them stand for 2 to 3 minutes, remove from oven, mix garlic and cover again. Cool.
4. Put salt, vinegar, chilies and garlic in a blender and blend till smooth.
5. In a small bowl heat oil for 2 minutes on micro High and mix with the smooth chili-garlic paste.
6. Transfer the sauce into a clean and dry glass bottle and store under refrigeration.

Usage: Chili-Garlic sauce is used for a variety of things while cooking. It can be mixed with gravies and can be added to flavour dry vegetables.

You may mix with sandwich spread to make yummy sandwiches.

You may use it along with salad dressings to flavour the vegetable salads.

Variation: Omit garlic and make 'Chili sauce'.

3. Brown Onion Paste

Micro Cooking: 30-40 mins

- Onion ...*1000 gm*
- Oil ... *3 tbsp*

Preparation and Cooking

1. Chop onions; mix with oil and cook in hot oven for 30 to 40 minutes or till it gets light brown in colour. Stir once.
2. Cool and pass through a liquidizer with ½ cup water for a slightly coarse paste.
3. Store in a clean tight jar under refrigeration. This paste lasts for 8 to 10 days.

Usage: Makes tastier vegetarian and non-vegetarian gravies in microwave without leaving behind a taste of uncooked onions.

Brown onion paste is very handy while cooking, and particularly while cooking in a microwave where we do not have the concept of frying (Bhuno) till oil separates. On the contrary, the oil does separate but with cooking for a specified period and using half done onion paste and giving proper standing time to the dish.

White Onion Paste can be prepared by cooking the onions with 1 cup water on micro High for 6 minutes. Cool and make a paste.

4. Basic White Sauce

Micro Cooking: 10 mins

✦ Milk	... *300 ml*	✦ Salt	... *½ tsp*
✦ Flour	... *1 tbsp*	✦ Pepper powder	...*½ tsp*
✦ Butter	... *1 tbsp*	✦ Mustard powder	...*¼ tsp*

Preparation and Cooking

1. Heat butter in a micro-safe bowl for 1 minute.
2. Add flour; stir and cook on micro High for 1 minute, uncovered.
3. Add milk and stir. Put a lid and cook on micro High i.e.100% power for first 2 minutes, stirring once and then on Medium, i.e. 80% power for 5 minutes, stirring twice in between with a hand beater/egg-beater.
4. Take out the dish and smell it. If a nice aroma of cooked flour is spreading around, that means sauce is ready, otherwise cook it for 1 minute more on micro High and let the dish stand for a couple of minutes, covered, to avoid formation of film on top.
5. Remove the lid and add salt, pepper and mustard powders. Stir properly and use.

Yield: This recipe will give you 1½ cups White Sauce.

Important: To make a nice and smooth sauce, it is important that all the ingredients used are at room temperature; how you are cooking it (in microwave or traditional way on gas heat, etc) is immaterial. However, if lumps are formed while cooking, pass the sauce through a liquidizer and then through a sieve. Sprinkle a little more milk and mix.

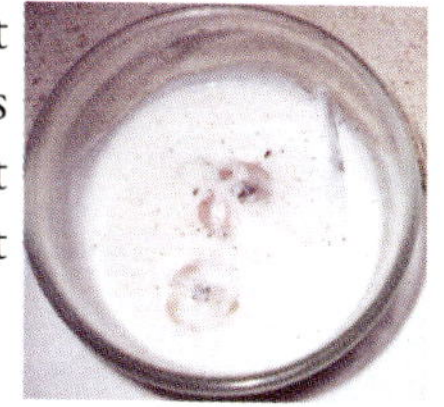

Note: Time taken is about 10 minutes micro cooking. On gas heat this sauce takes 20 minutes as it is cooked on slow fire with constant stirring.

Variation: Béchamel Sauce: White sauce flavoured with onion and cloves/nutmeg is called Béchamel Sauce. To get this, while making white sauce stick 3 cloves to a small peeled Onion and cook with sauce; once the sauce is cooked, gently, remove the onion and use sauce as required. Or flavour ready White Sauce with a pinch of Nutmeg powder (minus onion) and use.

Cheese Sauce: Add 3 tablespoon grated Cheese to the prepared hot White Sauce and mix to get Cheese Sauce. Do not cook again. Use it as and when required.

Mushroom Sauce: Take 1 recipe White Sauce and ¾ cup chopped Mushrooms, mix and cook on micro High for 2 minutes covered. Cool and pass through a liquidizer. Store under refrigeration and use it when required. Mix 2 tsp finely chopped Parsley/Coriander with it before serving.

Yield: Approximately 2 cups Mushroom sauce.

Tip: White Sauce/Béchamel Sauce/Cheese Sauce/ Mushroom Sauce can be stored under refrigeration for 2 to 3 days. Keep it covered in the chill tray of your refrigerator.

5. Szechuan Sauce

Micro Cooking: 8 mins

- Ginger chopped... *¼ cup*
- Oil ... *½ cup*
- Garlic chopped very fine ... *¼ cup*
- Red Chili powder ... *2 tbsp*
- Soy sauce ... *2 tsp*
- Sugar ... *1 tbsp*
- Salt ... *2 tbsp*
- Pepper powder ... *1 tsp*
- Vinegar ... *½ cup*

Preparation and Cooking

1. Grind ginger with vinegar to a fine paste.
2. Heat oil in a micro-safe bowl for 1 minute on High and add garlic and cook for 2 minutes on High, uncovered. Add ginger, stir it and cook on High for 2 minutes, uncovered, stirring once after 1 minute.
3. Add sugar, chili powder, soy sauce, salt and pepper; cover and cook for 3 minutes on Medium. Adjust salt if required. Cool and store. This sauce can last for many days under refrigeration.

Usage: Use this hot sauce for Chinese dishes; to enhance the taste of soups or to cook the hot and spicy dishes.

6. Mushroom Dip

Micro Cooking: 10 mins

- Mushrooms chopped ... *1 cup*
- Butter ... *2 tbsp*
- Flour ... *2 tbsp*
- Milk ... *500 ml*
- Salt ... *1 tsp*
- Mustard powder ... *¼ tsp*
- Pepper powder ... *1 tsp*

Preparation and Cooking

1. Make 1 recipe White sauce with butter, flour, milk, and season it with with salt, pepper and mustard powder.
2. Add 1 cup chopped mushrooms, mix and cook on micro High for 2 minutes covered.
3. Cool and pass through a blender. Store under refrigeration.
4. Mix 2 tsp finely chopped Parsley/Coriander with it before serving.

Yield: Approximately 2 cups Mushroom sauce.

Usage: Mushroom Dip is just ideal to be served with steamed Vegetables, grilled Chicken or Fish, Vegetable sticks, Soup sticks, Potato sticks or even with Potato or Corn wafers, etc, as starters.

7. Raw Mango Chutney/Chhunda

Micro Cooking: 10 mins

- Raw Mango... *1000 gm*
- Sugar ... *500 gm*
- Green Cardamom powder ... *2 tsp*
- Black Pepper powder ... *3 tsp*
- Salt (opt) ... *2 tbsp*

Preparation and Cooking

1. Wash, clean and grate the mangoes.
2. Place them in a large micro-safe bowl. Cover with a lid and micro cook on High for 6 minutes, stirring once in between.
3. Open the lid and put sugar and salt in cooked mangoes. Mix well and cover once again. Micro-cook on High for 5 minutes, so that sugar is dissolved.

4. Let the dish stand for 5 minutes; open the lid and sprinkle cardamom and pepper powders; mix well and cover the dish. Leave to cool. Mango chutney will turn out whitish green in colour.
5. Store in a clean jar. Lasts for months if kept properly under refrigeration.

Usage: Serve it with a variety of Rotis or use it for stuffing a Paratha.

Variation: Use Red Chili powder instead of pepper powder to get a reddish colour.

Tip: This preparation is very popular in North India.

8. Spicy Plum Sauce

Micro Cooking: 5 mins

- Plums ... *750 gm*
- Chili powder ... *1 tbsp*
- Sugar ... *1 cup*
- Salt ... *2 tbsp*
- Lemon juice ... *1 tbsp*
- Cinnamon ... *2" stick*
- Cloves ... *8 no*
- Black Cardamom ...*4 no*
- Nutmeg powder (opt) ... *¼ tsp*
- Peppercorns ... *12 no*
- Malt Vinegar/ Wine ... *¼ cup*

Preparation and Cooking

1. Wash and clean the plums. Cut and remove the stones.
2. Place them in a big glass bowl along with sugar, lemon juice and whole spices. Cover with the lid and micro cook for 5 minutes or till tender.
3. Cool slightly and pass through a liquidizer, sieve through a strainer, stir with a wooden spoon, collect the pulp and discard the roughage.

4. Now mix salt, nutmeg powder and vinegar/wine. Stir properly and adjust the seasoning.
5. Store it in a clean glass jar under refrigeration. The sauce can last long if every time a clean and dry spoon is used to take out the required quantity.

Usage: Serve this spicy plum sauce with Parathas/Poories or spread on Pancakes and Bread slices.

Tip: It is better to buy ripe plums for this sauce or you may have to adjust sugar according to your taste.

Nutmeg is optional in this recipe because its strong flavoured is not enjoyed by all.

9. Sweet-N-Sour Tamarind Sauce (Sonth)

Micro Cooking: 20 mins

- Tamarind ... *200 gm*
- Jaggery ... *300 gm*
- Dry Dates ... *10-15 no*
- Ginger powder ... *1 tbsp level*
- Red Chili powder ... *1 tbsp heap*
- Rock Salt powder ... *1 tbsp level*
- Salt ... *to taste*

- Fresh Mint ... *¼ cup*

Or

- Mint powder ... *1 tsp*

Preparation and Cooking

1. Wash tamarind and soak it along with jaggery in 2 cups water for 1 hour. Meantime soak dry dates for 30 minutes and micro cook on High for 2 minutes. Cool and remove the stones from dates and chop them roughly.
2. Transfer tamarind, jaggery and dates in a big micro-safe bowl, cover with the lid and cook on micro High for 10 minutes.

3. Cool, mash tamarind with your hands and strain through a sieve.
4. Collect the pulp in another bowl and mix rest of the ingredients in it.
5. Stir and cook on micro Low, that is 40% power for 8 minutes. Cool.
6. Adjust salt if at all required and store in a clean and dry glass bottle under refrigeration.

Note: This sweet and sour sauce lasts for months if properly stored.

Always take out the sauce in small quantity or as much as required for use and never mix the used one again with the stored lot.

Usage: This sauce is used all over India as an accompaniment to snacks and to enhance the flavour of steamed or fried Wadas in Curd (Dahi Wada), Chaat, Bhel and Pani Poori, etc.

Variation: Make **Sour Sauce of Tamarind.** Do not use jaggery but cook the same way with salt and other spices. Adjust salt if required.

Make **Sweet Sauce of Tamarind.** Instead of dry dates, use 200 gm Jaggery and ½ cup Raisins. Wash and use raisins. Rest follow the same recipe.

Breakfast

You must start your day with a good breakfast. As it is invariably the first meal of the day taken after a long interval, it is most important to balance it with proteins, carbohydrates and fibre.

It is said, one must eat breakfast like a king, lunch like a common man and dinner like a pauper. Keeping this saying in mind, popular healthy and nutritious breakfast dishes from Indian and International cuisine have been selected here. There is no dearth of dishes for breakfast but a few simple ones of universal appeal included in this section are cooked in your microwave oven with amazing ease.

1. Rava Idli

Micro Cooking: 10 mins **Serves: 4-6 persons**

- Rava/Semolina ...*1½ cups*
- Curd ... *3 cups*
- Asafetida ... *¼ tsp*
- Turmeric ... *½ tsp*
- Coriander chopped ... *¼ cup*
- Ginger grated ... *1 tsp*
- Coconut grated ...*¼ cup*
- Cashew nut bits roasted ... *2 tbsp*
- Mustard seeds ... *1 tsp*
- Pepper powder ... *1 tsp*
- Salt ... *1 tbsp or more*
- Ghee/Oil ... *1½ tbsp*

Preparation and Cooking

1. Roast semolina in a paper bag on micro High for 3 minutes, shaking once in between. Remove and take it out in a plate.
2. Beat curd with salt, pepper, asafetida and turmeric powder. Add chopped coriander, grated ginger, coconut, bits of cashew nuts and roasted semolina.

3. Heat ghee in a small micro-safe bowl for 30 seconds, add mustard seeds and microwave on High for 2 minutes.
4. Pour it over the semolina mix, stir properly and let it stand (soaked) for 30 to 40 minutes.
5. Smear the specially designed plastic idli moulds with a little oil and put 1 tbsp of batter in each depression. Put ¼ cup water in the container, place the mould stand in it, cover with lid and cook on micro High for 4 minutes.

Serving: Serve hot with Coconut Chutney/Green Chutney/Tomato Sauce.

Variation: Steam plain idlies with Idli batter available in the market the same way for same time. Or soak 2 cups Rice and 1 cup Urad dal separately for 4 hours. Grind the dal into a very smooth paste and the rice to a coarse paste; mix them well, add 1 tsp Salt and leave it at a warm place for fermentation overnight; in the hot weather the batter will be ready for breakfast the next morning; add a pinch of cooking Soda and 1 tbsp Oil, mix it well and steam idlies the above-mentioned way.

Vegetable Idlies: Add 1 cup finely diced Carrots, slivered Beans, shelled green Peas, finely cut green Chilies or Capsicums and Onion to the plain idli batter and steam.

Tip: The lightest, fluffy breakfast item 'Idli' of South India is made in various ways. This oil-free and low calorie food is a favourite of the young and old alike.

2. Vegetable Vermicelli

(Namkeen Sevian)

Micro Cooking: 15 mins **Serves: 4-6 persons**

- Vermicelli ... *2 cups*
- Beans thinly sliced ... *½ cup*
- Carrots juliennes... *¼ cup*
- Capsicum strips thinly cut ... *½ cup*
- Green Peas shelled ... *½ cup*
- Ghee/Oil ... *3 tbsp*
- Spring Onions sliced with greens ... *3 no*
- Green Chilies sliced lengthwise ... *3 no*
- Ginger juliennes... *2 tbsp*
- Tomato puree ... *¼ cup*
- Salt ... *to taste*
- Coriander chopped for garnishing

Preparation and Cooking

1. Roast vermicelli in a paper bag in microwave for 3 minutes on High, shaking once in between. Remove.

2. Heat oil in a big micro-safe bowl for 1 minute; add onion and cook for 2 minutes on High.

3. Add chopped vegetables; stir well to coat with oil and stir-fry on High for 4 minutes, stirring once.

4. Remove the bowl; sprinkle roasted vermicelli evenly over the vegetables; add salt, ginger and tomato puree; mix gently; sprinkle ¼ cup water and cook on micro High for 5 to 6 minutes, covered. Let the dish stand for 3 minutes.

Serving: Open the lid and loosen vermicelli with a fork; garnish with chopped Coriander and serve hot with Tomato sauce or fresh Green Chutney.

Variation: Instead of vermicelli use Rice Noodles but half boil them (like noodles) before adding to the vegetables.

3. Fluffy Omelet

Micro Cooking: 3 mins **Serves: 4-6 persons**

- Eggs ... *3 no*
- Butter ... *1 tbsp*
- Water ... *1 tbsp*
- Cream of Tartar... $^1/_8$ *tsp*
- Pie Plate for cooking omelet ...*9" in diameter*

Preparation and Cooking

1. Separate the egg yolks and whites.
2. Place the butter in a 9-inch pie plate; cook on High for 30 seconds to 1 minute or until melted.
3. Combine the egg whites and cream of tartar in a mixing bowl, beating until stiff but not dry.
4. In another small bowl mix together egg yolks and water, stirring until thick and lemon coloured; gently fold the yolks into the whites.

5. Pour the egg mixture into the pie plate with melted butter and spread smoothly with a spatula.
6. Cook on High for 2 to 2½ minutes or until set.
7. Score the omelet down the centre with a knife; fold and slide it onto the serving dish.

Note: Salt is not added to the omelet because it will reduce the elasticity which is required for volume.

Serving: Serve hot with any kind of Sauce and Bread.

Variation: The look of this omelet is whitish, so for the traditional pale brown look, a pinch of turmeric and a dash of chili sauce can be added to the beaten egg.

Add 2 to 3 tbsp of any prepared filling eg, Mushroom, Onion-Cheese-Tomato, etc. before folding the omelet.

Tip: An omelet cooked in the microwave will not burn or darken on the bottom and it folds nicely and effortlessly, too. Make sure to use the correct sized dish.

4. Sabudana Khichdi

Micro Cooking: 15-20 mins　　Serves: 4-6 persons

- Sabudana/Sago ... *2 cups*
- Peanuts ... *½ cup*
- Potatoes ... *2 no*
- Green Chilies ... *3 no*
- Coriander chopped ... *¼ cup*
- Lemons ... *2 no*
- Cumin ... *1 tsp*
- Cooking oil ... *¼ cup*
- Salt ... *2 tsp/to taste*
- Turmeric (opt) ... *1 tsp*
- Fresh Coconut grated (opt) ... *¼ cup*

Preparation and Cooking

1. Soak sago for 6 hours or overnight. For that wash sago and drain, keep it in a big bowl or a colander. Keep sprinkling water every 2 hours and mix it lightly, and use it after 6 hours of soaking. Otherwise soak it in the evening, keep sprinkling water and place in the refrigerator at night, and take it out 1 hour before use.

2. Roast peanuts on micro High for 2 minutes, cool and grind coarsely.
3. Peel and chop potatoes into small cubes and micro cook on High for 3 minutes, stand for 1 minute and take out from the micro oven. Keep aside, covered.
4. Chop green chilies. Squeeze juice from the lemons.
5. Heat oil in a micro-safe big bowl and put cumin, green chilies, coarsely ground peanuts, and turmeric; micro cook on High for 2 minutes, uncovered.
6. In the meantime mix together soaked sabudana, salt, lemon juice and cooked potatoes; add these to the oil and peanut mixture; stir lightly and cover the dish with a lid or cling film.
7. Pierce in the centre of the cling film and cook on micro High for 7 to 8 minutes. Stir once in between.
8. Give a standing time of 3 minutes and remove the dish from the oven.

Note: Do not sprinkle water over sabudana while placing it for cooking.

Serving: Sprinkle chopped coriander and grated coconut, loosen sabudana khichdi with a fork and serve hot with fresh Green Chutney or sweetened Curd.

Tip: This Khichdi is very popular in Maharashtra. It is available on bus stands and railway stations on Mondays, Thursdays and Saturdays when people are fasting.

5. Green Peas Poha

(Pressed Rice Preparation)

Micro Cooking: 11 mins **Serves: 4-6 persons**

◆ Poha	... *2 cups*	◆ Turmeric	... *1 tsp*
◆ Onion	... *1 no*	◆ Green Chilies	... *3 no*
◆ Lemon big	... *1 no*	◆ Cooking oil	... *3 tbsp*
◆ Green Peas	... *1 cup*	◆ Peanuts (opt)	... *¼ cup*
◆ Mustard seeds	... *1 tsp*	◆ Coriander chopped	... *¼ cup*
◆ Cumin	... *½ tsp*	◆ Salt	... *to taste*
◆ Curry leaves	... *1 sprig*		

Preparation and Cooking

1. Wash poha and keep in a colander/sieve for water to drain.
2. Chop onion lengthwise. Finely cut green chilies. Squeeze juice from the lemon.

3. Put oil, cumin, mustard seeds, green chilies and curry leaves in a large micro-safe bowl and microwave on High for 3 minutes, uncovered.
4. Add chopped onions, peanuts and turmeric powder; mix and microwave on High for 2 minutes.
5. Place green peas in the steaming basket with ½ tsp salt and ¼ cup water underneath and cook on High for 3 minutes and remove.
6. Finally add poha, green peas, lemon juice and salt to the big bowl with onions; mix properly with a light hand, sprinkle half the coriander on top, cover with a lid and cook on micro High for 4 minutes.
7. Give a standing time of 2 minutes, remove and garnish with rest of the coriander. Loosen it with a fork if necessary before serving.

Important: If quantity of the dish is larger, give 2 minutes more for cooking after final mixing. Rest of the procedure and the timings will remain same.

Serving: Serve hot with Green Chutney or a Sauce.

Variation: Instead of only green peas you may add 1 cup finely chopped Carrots, Potatoes and Capsicums.

Tip: It is a dry dish like rice pulao. So any chutney or sauce makes an excellent accompaniment. It can be easily carried in the tiffin box also.

Poha is a favourite breakfast dish of Maharashtrians and it is available on most of the Maharashtrian food stalls.

6. Grilled Cheese Toasts

Micro Cooking: 5-6 mins **Serves: 4-6 persons**

- Sandwich Bread ...*16 slices*
- Cheese grated ... *2 cups*
- Butter ... *½ cup*
- Milk ... *2 tbsp*
- Green Chilies chopped ... *6 no*
- Coriander chopped ... *¼ cup*
- Pepper powder ... *1 tsp*

Preparation and Cooking

1. Mix butter and cheese together in a micro-safe bowl, cover and soften in microwave for 30 to 40 seconds.
2. Take out and immediately mix rest of the ingredients thoroughly with a fork. Add a few drops of milk if too thick to be applied on the bread.
3. Spread evenly on all the slices.
4. Place 3 to 4 slices at a time on the stand and put it under the grill of your micro oven.

5. Press the Grill button and grill each lot for 5 to 6 minutes or till cheese spreads nicely and turns golden brown. Remove.

Serving: Cut the grilled toasts into triangles and serve them hot with Tomato sauce or fresh Green Chutney at breakfast time/with evening tea or with hot Soup or Stew at supper or dinner.

Cut them into small triangles and serve as one of the starters at any party.

Variation: Make **Garlic Toasts:** With ½ cup yellow butter mix 1 tbsp garlic paste or fresh nicely minced garlic and ¼ tsp pepper powder thoroughly; apply thinly on the bread and grill.

Tip: Do not add salt to the cheese and butter mixture if you are using yellow butter. If fresh home-made butter or cream (malai) is used with grated cheese, then you must add a large pinch of salt to the mixture.

7. Upma from Wheat Rava

Micro Cooking: 20 mins **Serves: 4-6 persons**

- Upma Rava ... *2 cups*
- Moong Sprouts... *1 cup*
- Raisins ... *¼ cup*
- Cashew nuts ... *¼ cup*
- Mustard seeds ... *1 tsp*
- Curry leaves ... *12 no*
- Red Chilies whole...*2 no*
- Green Chilies chopped ... *2 no*
- Carrot chopped ...*1 no* (optional)
- Roasted Gram dal ... *1 tbsp*
- Cooking oil ... *4 tbsp*
- Lemon juice ... *2 tbsp*
- Buttermilk ... *1 cup*
- Water ... *3 cups*
- Coriander chopped ... *2 tbsp*

Preparation and Cooking

1. Roast rava in a paper bag on micro High for 3 to 4 minutes, shaking it once in between. Remove and place in a plate.

2. Clean and soak raisins in water.
3. Roast cashew nuts in a paper bag on High for 2 minutes.
4. Put cooking oil in a deep micro-safe bowl; add mustard seeds, curry leaves, red chilies and roasted gram dal. Cook on micro High for 3 minutes, uncovered.
5. Add moong sprouts, carrot, green chilies and 1 tsp salt to it. Mix; cover the dish with a lid and cook on micro High for 3 minutes.
6. Remove and add roasted rava, lemon juice, buttermilk, 3 cups water, soaked raisins and salt to taste. Mix properly and cover it with a lid. Cook on micro High for 8 to 10 minutes.
7. Let the dish stand for 2 to 3 minutes.
8. Loosen it with a fork if required.

Serving: Garnish with chopped Coriander and roasted Cashew nuts. Serve it hot with Coconut Chutney/Green Chutney/Tomato Sauce, etc.

Variation: Vegetable Upma can be cooked with 2 cups chopped and boiled mixed vegetables and just ½ a cup roasted rava and 1 cup water. Rest use the same other ingredients.

Peanuts can be used in place of cashew nuts.

Pure Ghee can substitute cooking oil.

Tip: During monsoons or in a place with more humidity (like Mumbai), it is advisable to roast rava before storing.

Upma is a favourite breakfast dish in Southern and Western India. People of Maharashtra, Karnataka, Tamilnadu, Chennai and Andhra Pradesh love it.

8. Uttapum

Micro Cooking: 3 mins **Serves: 4-6 persons**

- Idli/Dosa batter...*500 gm*
- Oil ... *2 tbsp*
- Salt ... *2 tsp*
- Onion finely chopped ... *1 cup*
- 9-inch pie plates... *2 no*
- Tomato finely chopped ... *1 cup*
- Coriander chopped ... *½ cup*
- Green Chilies finely chopped ... *4 no*

Note: Dosa batter should be at room temperature.

Preparation and Cooking

1. Smear pie plates with a little oil.
2. Mix all the chopped vegetables and 1 tsp oil together.
3. Add 1½ tbsp oil and salt to the batter and mix well.
4. Pour ¼ cup batter in the pie plate; sprinkle a handful of chopped vegetables evenly over it; cook on micro High for 2½ minutes; stand for 2 minutes and transfer it with a spatula to the serving plate or to a casserole to keep it warm. Finish making all the uttapums this way.

Serving: Serve with Coconut Chutney.

Tip: Traditionally uttapums are made with a dosa batter that is a little more fermented, and are generally shallow fried, but our microwave uttapums turn out very good and healthly.

Coconut Chutney:

Roast 2 tbsp each gram dal + peanuts, 4 red chilies, few curry leaves in a paper bag on High for 2 minutes, shaking once in between. Cool and grind to a fine powder. Add 1 grated coconut + 1 cup curd and grind to a paste. Add 2 tsp tamarind pulp mixed with ¼ cup water and adjust salt. Heat a little oil in a ladle, crackle mustard in it; switch off the heat; mix ¼ tsp asafetida in oil and pour over chutney.

9. Kheema Mutter

(Mutton Mince and Green Peas)

Micro Cooking: 20 mins **Serves: 4-6 persons**

- Mutton mince... *500 gm*
- Onion-Tomato paste ... *½ cup*
- Ginger-Garlic paste ... *1 tbsp*
- Tomato puree ... *½ cup*
- Garam masala ... *1 tsp*
- Kashmiri Tikki masala ... *¼ cake*
- Salt ... *to taste*
- Red Chili powder (opt) ... *1 tsp*
- Dry Mint powder ...*1-2 tsp*
- Green Peas shelled ... *1-1½ cups*
- Cooking oil ... *¼ cup*
- Coriander chopped ... *¼ cup*

Preparation and Cooking

1. Heat oil in a micro-safe bowl for 1 minute on High; add mutton mince and mint powder; stir well to coat the meat properly and cook on High for 6 minutes, uncovered, stirring twice in between so that meat should not form lumps.
2. Add onion-tomato paste and ginger-garlic paste; mix well and cook for 3 minutes, uncovered.
3. Add powdered Tikki masala to the meat mixture along with garam masala, chili powder, salt and half the coriander. Mix well; cover with a lid and cook on High for 3 minutes.
4. Now add green peas, tomato puree and 1-1½ cups water and micro cook for 7 minutes on High. Let the dish stand for 5 minutes.
5. Remove and check the seasoning.

Serving: Garnished with remaining Coriander, serve with Buns at breakfast/brunch.

Variation: For vegetarians, instead of mutton mince take 1 cup Soya granules and soak them in water for 30 minutes; discard the water and follow the recipe step by step.

10. Breakfast Sausages

Micro Cooking: 8 mins **Serves: 4-6 persons**

- Chicken Sausages ... *200 gm*
- Spring Onions ... *3 no*
- Green Chilies ... *2 no*
- Tomato puree ... *¼ cup*
- Oregano ... *½ tsp*
- Cooking oil/ Butter ... *1 tbsp*
- Salt & Pepper... *to taste*
- Coriander or Parsley chopped for garnishing

Preparation and Cooking

1. Chop finely chilies and spring onions with greens.
2. Slice sausages into ¼-inch thick circles.
3. Heat fat in a micro-safe bowl for 1 minute on High and cook onions and chilies for 2 minutes on High, uncovered, stirring once in between.
4. Add sliced sausages, tomato puree, oregano, salt and pepper; stir well; cover with a lid and cook on High for 5 minutes.
5. Stand the dish for 2 minutes; open and garnish.

Serving: Serve hot on toasted Bread or with Buns or Parathas.

11. Dalia (Broken Wheat)

Micro Cooking: 20 mins **Serves: 4-6 persons**

◆ Dalia	... *1 cup*	◆ Milk	... *600 ml*
◆ Ghee	... *¼ cup*	◆ Raisins	... *¼ cup*
◆ Water	... *4 cups*	◆ Sugar	... *to taste*

Preparation and Cooking

1. Clean, wash and soak raisins in lukewarm water.
2. Place dalia in a paper bag and roast on micro High for 4 minutes, shaking once in between after 2 minutes.
3. Heat ghee in a deep micro-safe dish; mix roasted dalia with it; add raisins; pour 4 cups of water in it; cover with a lid and cook on micro High for 15 minutes.
4. Remove and stand the dish for 5 minutes. In the meantime heat milk on Reheat for 2 minutes in a micro-safe jug to be served with dalia.

Serving: Serve with hot milk and sugar to taste.

Variation: Add half milk and half water for cooking dalia.

Eat plain cooked dalia (without milk and raisins) with any curried vegetable or non-vegetarian preparation.

Tip: Dalia or porridge is a very healthy preparation for breakfast. It is full of protein and calcium. It is an excellent food for the young, old and pregnant women.

Porridge has been defined as a food made of oatmeal, wheat or some other cereal, boiled to a thick consistency in water or milk.

Soups and Salads

Soups not only provide nourishment to our body but also add variety to our meals. On a cold wintry night or a wet rainy day, soups lift our spirits. During hot summer months, cold soups work wonders. We take an almost complete mini meal in the form of soups and stews that contain vegetables, meats and condiments.

Salads have been defined as cold dishes consisting of certain raw vegetables covered with a dressing. Sometimes they may also contain seafood, meats and eggs. A salad dressing is usually with a base of salad oil or olive oil, vinegar or lemon juice, mayonnaise, cream, etc.

According to Indian food history, the Kachchdis, Pachchdis and Raitas fall in this category. They either have the curd base or the nut base and are tempered with oil, chilies, peppers and seeds.

Serve a bowl of salad and soup with meals and enjoy the goodness of fresh fruits and vegetables.

1. Hot Vegetable Stew

Micro Cooking: 17 mins **Serves: 4-6 persons**

- Baby Potatoes ... *12 no*
- Carrot cubed into ½" pieces ... *1 no large*
- Cauliflower cut into small pieces ... *1 cup*
- Green Pepper cut into ½" pieces ... *1 no small*
- Red Pepper cut into ½" pieces ... *1 small*
- Onion chopped into 1" pieces ... *1 no*
- Tomatoes ... *2 no*
- Cherry Tomatoes ...*12 no*
- Ginger-Garlic paste ... *1 tbsp*
- Mushrooms halved ... *1 cup*
- Red Chili whole ...*2 no*
- Peppercorns ... *12 no*
- Black Cardamoms...*3 no*
- Cinnamon ...*1" stick*
- Butter ... *2 tbsp*
- Flour/Corn flour ... *tbsp*
- Coriander/Parsley chopped ... *2 tbsp*
- Water ... *5 cups*

Preparation and Cooking

1. Cut tomatoes, pass through a liquidizer and strain the contents.
2. Clean and scrape the baby potatoes; combine with chopped carrots and cauliflower in the steaming basket; add ¼ cup water and cook on High for 3 minutes, covered.
3. Put butter in a large micro-safe bowl; heat for 1 minute on Reheat; add chopped onion, ginger-garlic paste; cook on micro High for 2 minutes.
4. Add whole spices, whole red chili and flour, mix and cook on High for 2 minutes, stirring once in between. Add the boiled vegetables to the bowl.
5. Add water/stock, tomato puree and salt; cover and cook on micro High for 7 minutes.
6. Open the lid and add chopped red and green peppers, cherry tomatoes and halved mushrooms. Cook for 2 minutes more on High.
7. Remove from microwave. Let the stew stand for 3 minutes; discard the whole chilies before serving.

Serving: Garnish with chopped fresh Coriander/Parsley and serve it hot with any kind of toasted Bread/ roasted Chapati, etc. A drop each of Soy sauce and Chili sauce can still be added to enhance the flavour.

Variation: Add cooked boneless Chicken or Mutton to it at step no 4 of cooking, and follow the rest of the process. Replace 2 cups water with Coconut milk and omit tomato puree completely.

Tip: This stew is a complete meal in itself.

2. Cream of Tomato Soup

Micro Cooking: 20 mins **Serves: 4-6 persons**

- Tomatoes ... *800 gm*
- Carrot ... *1 no*
- Ginger ... *1" piece*
- Garlic ... *6 flakes*
- Béchamel sauce ...*1½ cups*
- Pepper powder ... *1 tsp*
- Veg-Stock/ Water ... *3½ cups*
- Salt ... *to taste*
- Fresh Cream ... *¼ cup*
- Bread Croutons/Fried Phool Makhanas...*a few*

Preparation and Cooking

1. Cook roughly chopped tomatoes and carrot with ½ cup water on micro High for 5 minutes.
2. Cool and liquidize to puree consistency. Mix 2 cups stock and strain through a sieve.
3. Mix béchamel sauce with tomato mixture in a blender.
4. Place the mixture in a deep micro-safe bowl and add 1 cup stock, salt and pepper powder, and stir well.
5. Cook on micro High for first 5 minutes and then on Medium for 10 minutes. Remove; mix cream in it.

Serving: Serve hot in individual soup bowls/cups garnished with fried Phool Makhanas, i.e. roasted Lotus seeds, or roasted Bread Croutons.

Variation: Cream of Spinach: Spinach puree + White Sauce + Stock + fresh Cream + Seasoning.

Cream of Pumpkin: Cooked and pureed Pumpkin pulp + Asafetida powder + Bechamel Sauce + Seasoning. Serve it garnished with roasted Sesame seeds.

Cream of Mushroom: Mushroom Sauce passed through a liquidizer + veg/non-veg Stock + chopped Mushroom + Seasoning + Cream.

Cream of Mixed Vegetables: Cooked and pureed mix Vegetables + Ginger powder + Water + Seasoning + Coconut Milk. Add a Bouquet garni while cooking vegetables.

3. Chinese Chicken Corn Soup

Micro Cooking: 18 mins **Serves: 4-6 persons**

- Boneless Chicken breast ... *1 no*
- Cream style/Tender grated Corn ... *1½ cups*
- Water/Chicken stock ... *6 cups*
- Eggs ... *2 no*
- Corn flour ... *3 tbsp*
- Salt ... *to taste*

To serve with

- Soy sauce ... *2 tbsp*
- Green Chilies chopped ... *3 no*
- Table vinegar ... *¼ cup*
- Chili sauce ... *2 tbsp*

Preparation and Cooking

1. Put 5 cups chicken stock in a large deep micro-safe bowl; place corn and boneless chicken in it; cover with a lid and cook on micro High for 10 minutes.
2. Stand the dish for 3 minutes; take out chicken, cool and cut it neatly into thin strips or shred it.
3. Keep the soup warm. Mix corn flour with remaining 1 cup stock and pour into the hot soup. Add 1 tsp

salt and stir well. Cover and cook on micro High for 6 minutes or till it boils, stirring twice in between.

4. In the meantime beat eggs and pour into the hot soup through a rice strainer and keep stirring. Or pour the beaten eggs slowly from a height in a thin stream. Do not let the eggs coagulate.
5. Mix shredded chicken in the soup and heat through for 2 minutes on Reheat and serve.

Note: This soup is supposed to be thick in consistency, so if required you may increase quantity of corn flour.

Serving: Serve hot with the various Sauces. This is one of the most favourite Chinese soups relished by young and old alike, in India.

Variation: Cook Corn and Vegetable Soup with or without egg drops. Omit chicken and instead use 1½ cups chopped Vegetables, like Carrot, Cauliflower, Beans, Mushrooms and Capsicum along with Corn and follow the same procedure. Garnish with ¼ cup chopped Coriander and serve with various sauces.

Cook Shrimp, Chicken and Sweet Corn Soup without egg drops. Use 1 cup full kernel Corn, ½ cup shelled Shrimps, ½ cup green Peas and boneless Chicken breast meat. Flavour it with Black Pepper.

Cook Chicken Noodles Soup without egg drops. Omit corn, reduce the quantity of corn flour to 1 tbsp; add 1 cup instant broken Noodles and boil with shredded Chicken and Ham in the soup for 3 minutes.

It is said that Chinese Chicken Noodle Soup is served on festive occasions in China. There, each guest is given a bowl the moment he or she arrives, as much as the guests are served cocktails in the Western countries or beverages in India.

Tip: Do not put more Salt in the soup because Soy sauce is very salty in nature.

4. Pasta Slaw

Micro Cooking: 15 mins | Serves: 4-6 persons

- Instant Noodles ... *200 gm*
  Or
- Macaroni/Pasta ... *1 cup*
- Potato ... *1 no*
- Green Peas ... *1 cup*
- Tomato ... *1 no*
- Carrots ... *2 no*
- Red Pepper ... *1 no*
- Cucumber ... *1 no large*
- Celery sticks ... *2 no*
- Mushrooms ... *100 gm*
- Cabbage ... *8 leaves*
- Mayonnaise ... *½ cup*
- Mustard sauce ... *¼ cup*
- Tomato sauce ... *¼ cup*
- Fresh Cream ... *¼ cup* (optional)

Preparation and Cooking

1. Boil 4 cups water in a big bowl on micro High for 5 minutes and add macaroni, 1 tsp salt and 1 tsp oil. Cover and cook for 6 to 7 minutes or till soft. Instant noodles will take half the time to cook.

2. Remove and drain water, and run under the tap. Keep them covered.
3. Peel, wash and cut potato and carrots into small cubes and steam on micro High for 3 minutes. Let them stand for 2 minutes. Take them out and mix with macaroni.
4. Chop red pepper and celery in matchstick fashion.
5. Remove the spine of cabbage leaves, roll them tightly and shred finely. Soak cabbage in cold water for 30 minutes. Drain and keep cool under refrigeration.
6. For a greener effect slice cucumber thinly without peeling it. Also slice the tomato. Cut mushrooms into halves.

Assembling: Mix mushrooms, red pepper, celery, boiled vegetables and macaroni in a bowl; pour all the sauces over and toss once or twice or mix gently with a light hand and refrigerate salad for at least 30 minutes before serving.

Serving: Arrange cucumber and tomato slices on a large platter; lay cooled cabbage on top and then place the pasta salad in the centre. Or serve as you wish.

Starters and Evening Snacks

Basically, starters are bite-sized foods served before meals to stimulate the taste buds. Starters should be selected according to the main course menu. If the dishes for main course are heavy and filling in nature, the starters should be light so that main course can be enjoyed properly and vice versa if main course does not consist of heavy dishes. Moreover, if the main course is mainly non-vegetarian, the starters should be more vegetable based foods so that balance in meals can be maintained. Snacks selected for the cocktails or birthdays, etc, should be more filling as, generally, no main course is planned after that.

In this section, many popular and innovative starters and snacks have been included that can be easily cooked in the micro or convection mode of your micro oven.

1. Cheese Coins

Micro Baking: 15 mins **Serves: 4-6 persons**

- Bread slices ... *12 no*
- Paneer/Cottage cheese ... *1½ cup*
- Potato boiled ... *1 no*
- Flour ... *1 tbsp*
- White Pepper powder ... *2 tsp*
- Mint powder ... *½ tsp*
- Cheese grated ... *¼ cup*
- Red/Green Pepper ... *2" piece*
- Black Peppercorns ... *24 no*
- Salt ... *to taste*
- Baking tray ... *1 no*

Preparation and Cooking

1. Preheat the Convection mode of your microwave at 180° Celsius.
2. With the help of a biscuit cutter or a small cup/ katori cut 12 roundels out of bread slices.

3. Grind the remaining portions of slices in an electric grinder to make fresh breadcrumbs.
4. Cut the pepper into thin strips of ¾-inch long pieces.
5. Combine paneer, potato, breadcrumbs, flour, mint, salt and pepper powder in a bowl, stir well and knead the mixture to a fine dough.
6. Divide the dough into 12 portions.
7. Spread one portion of dough on 1 roundel of bread. Place 2 peppercorns as eyes and 1 strip of pepper like a mouth. In this way finish making all the roundels and place them in a baking tray.
8. Bake in hot oven for 10 to 15 minutes and remove.

Serving: Serve these happy looking faces hot or at room temperature with Tomato sauce as an evening snack.

You may serve them as starters at any gathering; in that case just remove the sides of bread slices, follow the rest of the procedure, place pepper corns in 4 corners and bake squares; later cut them into 4 portions each to make bite sized pieces and serve.

Tip: Cheese Coins are ideal for children's gatherings or birthday parties because they love shapes and crispness in any food.

2. Cauliflower and Peanut Cutlets

Micro Cooking: 8 mins **Grilling: 16 mins**

- Cauliflower grated ... *3 cups*
- Potatoes chopped ... *3 no*
- Peanuts roasted ... *¼ cup*
- Bread slices ... *2 no*
- Garam masala ... *1 tsp*
- Mango powder ... *1 tsp*
- Green Chilies chopped ... *3 no*
- Dry Fenugreek leaves ... *2 tbsp*
- Milk ... *2–3 tbsp*
- Salt ... *to taste*

Preparation and Cooking

1. Place grated cauliflower and chopped potatoes in a micro-safe bowl; sprinkle 2 tbsp water; cover and cook on micro High for 6 minutes. Stand the dish for 5 minutes.
2. Meantime place peanuts in a small paper bag and roast on High for 2 minutes, shaking once. Cool and powder coarsely.
3. Crumble bread in a grinder and make fresh breadcrumbs.
4. Mash cauliflower and potato well; add peanut powder, breadcrumbs, chilies and dry spices. Mix properly; sprinkle milk to moisten the mixture and knead.
5. Divide the mixture into 8 to 10 portions and shape like cutlets.
6. Put 2 tbsp oil in a flat dish; roll the cutlets to coat with oil and grill them on the high rack for 16 minutes, turning once after 7 minutes. Leave them under the grill for 5 minutes.

Serving: Serve with any Chutney or Sauce at teatime, or at a dinner, accompanied with a good Salad and Soup.

Variation: These cutlets can also be used as Burger Patties.

Replace peanuts by Moong sprouts in the recipe.

3. Cookies

Micro Baking: 10-15 mins **Serves: 4-6 persons**

✦ Flour	... *120 gm*	✦ Baking powder	... *¼ tsp*
✦ Butter	... *80 gm*	✦ Almond powder	...*2 tbsp*
✦ Powdered Sugar	...*80 gm*	✦ Baking tray	... *1 no*

Preparation and Cooking

1. Preheat the micro oven's Convection mode for 15 to 20 minutes at 180° Celsius.
2. Sieve flour and baking powder together.
3. Beat butter with hand.
4. Add powdered sugar and mix well.
5. Now put rest of the ingredients and knead well to make a pliable smooth dough.
6. Roll the dough into ¼-inch thick disc (chapati) and cut the cookies with a biscuit cutter.

7. Place them in a baking tray or on aluminium sheet on the turntable and bake for 10 to 15 minutes or till golden brown.
8. Remove the tray and cool.
9. Store them in an airtight container.

Serving: Serve with tea or any other beverage.

Variation: Instead of almond powder, use Pistachio nuts powder.

Note: Cookies or biscuits can't be baked in Microwave mode. They may be baked in Convection mode of microwave oven, OTG or cooking range.

4. Masala Dhokla

Micro Cooking: 15 mins — Serves: 4-6 persons

- Rice ... *1 cup*
- Chana/Gram dal...*½ cup*
- Urad/Black gram ...*¼ cup*
- Green Chilies ... *5 no*
- Ginger-Garlic paste ... *1 tbsp*
- Salt ... *1 tbsp*
- Turmeric ... *1 tsp*
- Onion-Tomato paste ... *½ cup*

Or

- Tomato sauce ... *¼ cup*
- Buttermilk ... *2 cups*
- Coconut grated... *½ no*
- Coriander ... *½ cup*
- Red Chilies ... *2 no*
- Mustard seeds ... *1 tsp*
- Oil ... *3 tbsp*
- Cooking soda/ Eno fruit salt ... *1½ tsp*

Preparation and Cooking

1. Clean, wash and soak chana dal, urad dal and rice in buttermilk for 4 hours.

2. Grind them to a smooth paste along with green chilies. Add ginger paste, salt, turmeric and cooking soda and keep for 6 to 8 hours. Make a batter of dropping consistency. If needed add ¼ cup water and mix well.

3. Use idli stand of microwave oven; put 1 tbsp batter in each depression; add ½ cup water in the steaming container and fit the stand in it and steam dhoklas for 3 to 4 minutes. Let it stand for 2 minutes and remove. This way finish steaming the dhokla idlies till the batter is finished.

4. Cut each idli into 4 pieces and keep aside, covered.

5. Heat 2 tbsp oil in a micro safe dish for 1 minute on High; add whole red chili and mustard seeds and cook for 2 minutes on High.

6. Add onion-tomato paste or tomato sauce, grated coconut, half of the coriander and ½ cup water; cover and cook for 2 minutes on High; mix the pieces of steamed dhokla, cover once again and heat through for 3 minutes on Reheat.

Serving: Serve hot as an evening snack or on toothpicks as a starter.

Note: If you do not have an idli stand, steam in a flat bowl.

Tip: This Gujarati dish, a popular snack, is available all over India these days. This recipe is one of the oldest developed ages ago.

5. Young Potatoes' Delight

Micro Cooking: 13 mins **Serves: 4-6 persons**

- Baby Potatoes ...*500 gm*
- Szechuan sauce ...*½ cup*
- Sesame seeds ... *2 tbsp*
- Coriander chopped ... *¼ cup*
- Toothpicks ... *20 no*

Preparation and Cooking

1. Steam potatoes on micro High for 8 minutes. Stand for 5 minutes and then rinse in tap water.
2. Peel the potatoes and prick them lightly with a fork.
3. Put sesame seeds in an envelope and roast on High for 2 minutes, shaking once in between.
4. Put Szechuan sauce and potatoes in a heatproof dish with a lid; stir gently, so that they are coated well with sauce. Heat through on Reheat for 3 minutes.
5. Open the lid and sprinkle potatoes with chopped coriander and sesame seeds.

Serving: Serve as starters or as a side dish with any meal.

Variation: Use leftover Mango Pickle masala instead of Szechuan sauce to coat potatoes with.

6. Veg & Non-veg Burger Patties

Micro Cooking: 7 mins   Serves: 4-6 persons

For Non-Veg Meat Patties

- Mutton mince... *600 gm*
- Onions finely chopped ... *¼ cup*
- Green Chilies finely chopped ... *3 no*
- Garam masala ... *1 tsp*
- Pepper powder ... *1 tsp*
- Ginger powder ... *½ tsp*
- Fresh Breadcrumbs ... *1 cup*
- Egg ... *1 no*
- Salt ... *to taste*
- Oil ... *¼ cup*

Preparation and Cooking

1. Combine together all the ingredients except oil and mash them well.
2. Divide the mixture into 6 equal parts and shape into 3-inch round patties.
3. Put oil in a flat micro safe dish and heat on High for 2 minutes and place the patties in oil and roll them to be coated with oil properly.

4. Cook on High for 3 minutes; turn the side and cook for 2 minutes. You may use them like this or grill them for 10 to 15 minutes.

Assemble the way veg burgers are described:

For Veg Burger Patties

- Soya Granules ... *1 cup*
- Potatoes boiled ... *3 no*
- Green Peas boiled... *1 cup*
- Onion chopped... *1 small*
- Green Chilies chopped ... *6 no*
- Coriander chopped ... *¼ cup*
- Pepper powder ... *1 tsp*
- Garam Masala ... *1 tbsp*
- Roasted Gram powder ... *½ cup*
- Fresh Breadcrumbs ... *1 cup*
- Egg ... *1 no*
- Oil ... *2 tbsp*
- Salt ... *to taste*
- Burger Buns ... *6 no*

Preparation and Cooking

1. Soak soya granules in water for 30 to 40 minutes; drain and squeeze; wash and squeeze again.

2. Combine soya, potatoes, peas, onion, chilies and egg in a grinder and grind coarsely.

3. Mix roasted gram powder, breadcrumbs, salt, coriander and other dry spices with soya paste thoroughly and divide into equal portions to shape 3-inch round patties.

4. Put oil in a flat micro safe dish and heat on High for 2 minutes; place the patties in the dish and roll to cover them with oil; cook on micro High for 2 minutes; turn the side and cook for 2 minutes on High. Stand the dish for 3 minutes.

6. You may use the patties cooked like this or grill them for 10 to 15 minutes, turning over after 5 minutes.

Assembling and Serving: Cut 6 burger buns into two parts, brown the inner side under the grill for 5 minutes; apply Tomato sauce on one side and Green Chutney on the other side and place the patties, one each, in the centre. Place a piece of lettuce, onion slice and tomato slice, too, in each burger. Cover with the other half; secure them with toothpicks and serve with additional Sauce and any of the Salads.

Tip: Soya granules are rich in protein that provides natural vitamins and minerals essential for children's growth. Since the soya preparations are low in cholesterol and fats, they are light and easy to digest; excellent for people on diet; expectant mothers, diabetics, heart patients and the aged, etc; any food lover can enjoy them with zest and zeal.

Burgers being the popular snacks of today's world, this option is being given here. Of course, you can use your popular potato patties, too, for making burgers.

Avoid: Using fried patties for making burgers for your growing children because with lots of fats, hardly any nutrition value is there. If you plan sensibly and provide good Salad and a Soup along with the burger, even this so-called junk fast food also provides nutrition.

7. Grilled Chana Kababs

(Bengal Gram Kababs)

Micro Cooking: 10-15 mins **Grilling: 20 mins**

- Bengal Gram ... *¾ cup*
- Green Chilies ... *4 no*
- Garlic flakes ... *12 no*
- Ginger powder ... *1 tsp*
- Garam masala ... *1 tsp*
- Peppercorns ... *12 no*
- Roasted Sesame seed powder ... *¼ cup*
- Egg ... *2 no*
- Salt ... *to taste*

Preparation and Cooking

1. Wash and soak Bengal gram/chana for 6 hours.
2. Drain the water and place gram in a micro-safe bowl along with green chili, peppercorns and garlic flakes. Add 1 tsp salt and 1 cup water.
3. Cover with a lid and boil for 15 minutes on High. Let the dish stand for 10 minutes.

4. Grind gram in electric mixer along with eggs, ginger powder and garam masala.
5. Remove and add sesame powder to it. Knead very well and check the salt.
6. Divide the mixture into lemon sized portions. Smear your palms with oil and roll each portion and flatten it. Finish rolling all the portions and place them on the grilling rack. Brush the kababs lightly with oil.
7. Grill the flattened kababs for 20 minutes, turning once after 10 minutes. Brush this side of kababs, too, with oil.

Serving: Arrange on a bed of lettuce with onion rings and serve as starters or evening snack with green Chutney/ Tomato Sauce or Yogurt Dip.

Yogurt Dip: Mix ½ cup Hung Curd with 1 tbsp chopped Coriander/Parsley, 1 tsp green Chili sauce and 1 tbsp grated Cheese. Add salt and pepper to taste. Chill before serving.

8. Steamed Corn on the Cob

Micro Cooking: 5 mins | Serves: 4-6 persons

- Corn on the cob ... *4 no*

Preparation and Cooking

1. Clean and wash corn cobs; place in steaming basket and put ¼ cup water. Steam on High for 5 minutes. If cobs are too big, cut them into two.

Serving Options:

1. Corn on the Cob: Cut lemon; dip in the salt and rub on steamed corns and serve immediately.
2. Spicy Corn on the Cob: Cut corn on cobs into pieces, apply Tomato sauce/Chutney and serve.
3. Cheesy Corn: Cut into two lengthwise; arrange in a heatproof dish; evenly sprinkle grated cheese and pepper powder. Grill for 5 minutes, and serve hot.
4. Corn on the Cob Au Gratin: Brush steamed corn with melted butter; roll in grated cheese and bake in hot oven for 10 minutes.

9. Patod or Aadoo Wadi

(Colocasia leaves Steamed Rolls)

Micro Cooking: 5 mins **Serves: 4-6 persons**

- Colocasia leaves ... *8–12 no*
- Gram flour ... *2 cups*
- Salt ... *2 tsp*
- Chili powder ... *1 tsp*
- Chili sauce ... *1 tsp*
- Ginger-Garlic paste ... *1 tsp*
- Water ... *1 cup or as much as required*
- Oil ... *1 tbsp*
- Mustard seeds ... *1 tsp level*

Preparation and Cooking

1. Mix together gram flour, salt, chili powder, ginger-garlic paste, chili sauce and 1 cup water to form a smooth paste of applying consistency. Add a little more water (if required) to get the right consistency. Keep it away for 15 minutes.

2. Meantime wash colocasia leaves and wipe them dry with a kitchen duster. Cut the stems and discard.
3. Place one leaf on the working place and apply the gram flour paste on it generously. Place another one on top and apply the paste. In this way repeat the process with 4 to 6 leaves. Now start rolling it tightly in a cylindrical shape. Repeat the process with rest of the leaves.
4. Arrange them in the steaming basket and steam for 5 minutes. Give standing time of 3 minutes.
5. Remove the steamed rolls and place them on the chopping board. Cool a little and slice them into ½-inch thick slices.
6. Heat oil in a pan on the top of the gas stove; crackle mustard seeds in it and mix the chopped rolls with mustard seeds. Turn the side gently; take out and arrange in a shallow dish.

Serving: Serve as a snack/starter with Tomato sauce or as a side dish with any meal.

Variation: After slicing the steamed rolls deep-fry them in hot oil.

Tip: In the Western and Southern side of India, this preparation is eaten in the form of steamed and tempered rolls and is called 'Aadoo Wadi', whereas in Northern part and Central India this is relished in the fried form and is called 'Patod'.

Colocasia leaves are known as Arvi-Ka-Patta/Aadoo.

10. Spicy Nuts

Micro Cooking: 4-5 mins **Serves: 4-6 persons**

- Almonds shelled ... *1 cup*
- Butter ... *2 tbsp*
- Worcestershire sauce ... *2 tbsp*
- Salt ... *½ tsp*
- Chili-Garlic sauce ... *1 tsp*
- Cinnamon powder ... *¼ tsp*
- Clove powder ... *a pinch*

Preparation and Cooking

1. Place butter in the rectangular dish; heat for 1 minute on High and stir in the sauces and dry ingredients except almonds.
2. Stir in the almonds, coating well; cook on High for 4 to 5 minutes, uncovered, stirring once after 2 minutes.
3. Cool and store in airtight jar; the nuts stay fresh at room temperature for about 2 weeks to 1 month.

Serving: Serve as starters in the winter months or enjoy them any time.

Variation: Spice up Walnuts or Peanuts.

Main Course

A wide variety of Indian and International cuisine has been carefully chosen. These vegetarian and non-vegetarian dishes for the main course are not only nutritious but also appeal to our tastes. Although the growing liking for various cosmopolitan foods has inspired me to include more number of vegetable and meat-based dishes, yet proper guidelines have been given to cook lentils, rice and pasta, that are the backbone of any cuisine. Intentionally, an ease in cooking any cuisine is developed so that any proud owner of a microwave, sitting at home, can enjoy or serve at least 'a three-course meal' in style to his or her family and friends. Special care is taken in explaining the serving of the dishes with their proper accompaniments, so that at the end of the show even a beginner or a keen learner of cooking also succeeds in his or her efforts, because as the saying goes — nothing succeeds like success.

1. Brinjal Canoes

Micro Cooking: 35 mins **Serves: 4-6 persons**

- Brinjal large ... *2 no*
- Paneer grated ... *1 cup*
- Green Peas ... *1 cup*
- Spring Onions with greens ... *3 no*
- Chili paste ... *1 tsp*
- Ginger paste ... *1 tsp*
- Tomato puree ... *¼ cup*
- Red Pepper ... *¼ of pepper*
- Cheese grated ... *2 tbsp*
- Egg ... *1 no*
- Mixed Spice ... *1 tsp*
- Roasted Cumin powder ... *½ tsp*
- Pepper powder ... *½ tsp*
- Oil ... *2 tbsp*

Preparation and Cooking

1. Cut brinjals lengthwise into two parts; smear a little oil on the inside and outside. Place on the microwave turntable in a ring form with thicker portions outwards and cook on micro High for 5 minutes.

2. Take them out; cool slightly and scoop out the pulp, leaving ½" thick layer inside.
3. Chop pulp, spring onions and their greens. Cut red pepper into tiny pieces, save one strip for garnishing.
4. Heat oil in a micro-safe bowl for 1 minute on High; add chopped onions and cook on High for 2 minutes, uncovered; add salt, chili and ginger pastes, chopped pulp and green peas; mix well and cook on High for 4 minutes, covered with a lid.
5. Now add tomato puree, red pepper, paneer and dry spices. Cover and cook for 3 minutes on High. Beat egg and mix with it.
6. Stuff the brinjal shells with this mixture; sprinkle grated cheese on top and garnish with red pepper.
7. Place them in a heatproof plate and cook on Combination-1 mode for 20 minutes. The top should be golden brown.

Serving: Serve hot with any Indian or Continental meal.

Variation: Stuff the canoes with minced Chicken or Mutton. Precook the mince and mix with the brinjal pulp and peas at step no 6 of cooking; omit paneer totally and continue cooking.

Tip: Canoes/boats can be stuffed and kept in refrigerator, covered with foil or cling film. But they should be taken out beforehand for baking.

2. Masala Arvi

Micro Cooking: 18-20 mins **Serves: 4-6 persons**

- Arvi/Colocasia... *1000 gm*
- Tomato puree ... *¾ cup*
- Ajwain ... *1 tsp*
- Mint powder ... *1 tsp*
- Chili-Garlic sauce ... *3 tbsp*
- Cooking oil ... *3 tbsp*
- Mixed Spice powder ... *1 tsp*
- Salt ... *2 tsp or to taste*
- Coriander chopped ... *¼ cup*

Preparation and Cooking

1. Wash and place arvi in the steaming basket and microwave on High for 8 minutes; remove from the oven and stand for 5 minutes; peel and keep aside.
2. Put oil in a micro-safe dish; add ajwain to it and crackle on High for 2 minutes, uncovered. Add tomato puree, chili-garlic sauce, mint powder, salt and mixed spice powder to it. Now cook for 3 minutes, covered.
3. Add arvi to the tomato mixture; stir well; cover and cook on micro High for 5 minutes.
4. Stand it for 2 to 3 minutes.

Serving: Garnish with chopped coriander and serve it with hot Phulkas/Parathas or with Dal-Rice.

Variation: Instead of arvi use boiled Potatoes. Use Paneer pieces but just heat it through after adding to cooked tomato and chili mixture. Reheat for 2 minutes. Over-cooking makes Paneer leathery.

Tip: Arvi can be boiled and peeled in advance. Its gravy also can be prepared in advance. Final dish can be assembled and heated through for 7 to 8 minutes just before serving.

3. Malai Koftas in Quick Gravy

(Steamed Malai Koftas)

Micro Cooking: 18 mins   Serves: 4-6 persons

For Koftas:

- Paneer grated ... *1½ cups*
- Mawa/Khoya ... *½ cup*
- Mixed Nuts chopped ... *¼ cup*
- Corn flour ... *2 tbsp*
- Basil leaves chopped ... *8 to 10*
- White Pepper powder ... *2 tsp*
- Salt ... *to taste*

For Quick Gravy:

- Tomato puree ... *400 ml*
- Butter ... *100 ml*
- Cream ... *200 ml*
- Khoya/Mawa ... *25 gm*
- Ginger paste ... *1 tbsp*
- Cumin ... *1 tsp*
- Cloves ... *6 no*
- Red Chili powder ... *1 tbsp*
- Garam masala ... *1 tbsp*
- Coriander leaves chopped ...*¼ cup*

Preparation and Cooking

1. Mix together all the ingredients for koftas; divide the mixture into 12 portions; roll them and place in the steaming basket; steam on High for 3 minutes. Let them stand for 4 minutes.
2. Heat butter in a big micro-safe bowl for 1 minute on High. Add cumin and coriander and cook on High for 2 minutes.
3. Add ginger paste, tomato puree, red chili powder, mixed spice and salt to the bowl, cover and cook on High for 6 minutes.
4. Add cream and mawa and cook on Medium for 6 minutes. Let the dish stand for 10 minutes and then serve.

Serving: In a shallow heatproof dish arrange steamed koftas and pour gravy over them just before serving. Cover the dish with cling film or a cover and heat through on Reheat for 3 to 4 minutes and serve with Phulkas/ Parathas or Naan, etc.

Variation: Quick gravy can also be combined with any other Koftas/Meatballs/cubed Paneer or boiled Peas and Mushrooms, etc.

Try making **Raw Banana Koftas:** Steam 2 raw bananas with skin for 4 minutes; peel and mash with 2 tbsp corn flour; season with spices; stuff with 50 gm mawa; roll and steam for 2 minutes and place in gravy.

Tip: This gravy may appear rich and heavy due to cream and mawa, but once combined with steamed koftas, it balances very well.

4. Sarson-Ka-Saag

(A Pungent and Tasty Relish of Brassica leaves)

Micro Cooking: 30-35 mins **Serves: 4-6 persons**

- Sarson leaves ...*1000 gm*
- Spinach/Cholai...*500 gm*
- Onion ... *1 no large*
- Tomato ... *1 no large*
- Ginger ... *2" piece*
- Garlic paste ... *1 tbsp*
- Green Chilies ... *4 no*
- Red Chili powder ...*1 tsp*
- Pure Ghee ... *3 tbsp*
  Or
- Butter ... *4 tbsp*
- Corn meal ... *2 tbsp*

Preparation and Cooking

1. Clean the sarson (mustard) leaves and peel the stems. Wash and chop the leaves roughly. Cut the stems into small pieces.

2. Clean and wash spinach leaves and cut them, too. Chop onion, tomato and green chilies very fine. Grate ginger and keep aside.

3. Put mustard leaves and stems in a large micro-safe bowl and cover it with a lid. Cook on micro High for 10 minutes, stirring after five minutes. Let the dish stand for 5 minutes and cool slightly.

4. In another bowl cook spinach for 5 minutes on micro High and cool.

5. Mix them together and pass through a blender to make a smooth paste. Do not add extra water.

6. In the large bowl heat 2 tbsp ghee or 3 tbsp butter for 1 minute on High and add chopped onion and garlic. Cook on micro High for 3 minutes, uncovered; stirring once in between. Remove the dish and add chopped tomato, chilies and ginger; cook on micro High for 2 minutes, uncovered and remove.

7. Add corn meal and chili powder, mix and cook for 1 minute, uncovered.
8. Mix the paste of mustard and spinach leaves with the tempering masala; add salt; cover and cook on micro High for 10 minutes, stirring once in between.
9. Remove the lid and stir; if the preparation seems a little watery, cook it uncovered for 5 minutes on micro High and let it stand uncovered for 30 minutes. You may reheat it before serving.

Serving: Add 1 tbsp remaining ghee or butter on top of saag and serve it piping hot with Corn meal bread (Makki-ki-Roti) or Wheat Chapati, etc.

Variation: Instead of spinach mix other greens like Turnip and Radish leaves with the mustard leaves and cook the same way.

Tip: Cooking Sarson Ka Saag is really very practical in the microwave. In conventional cooking you spend almost 2 hours to cook this pungent and tasty dish. If you like you may save more time by preparing tempering on the gas stove. Final 10 minutes cooking can be done just before serving.

Information: 'Acaranga Sutra' has mentioned that the use of Brassica leaves as a tasty relish, now consumed as Sarson ka Saag, was first noted around 500 BC.

It is believed that since North Indians consume so much of green leaves in the form of Saags, their bodies keep getting good doses of Chlorophyll essential for the human system.

5. Stuffed Bottle Gourd

Micro Cooking: 24 mins **Serves: 4-6 persons**

- ✦ Tender Bottle Gourd ... *600 gm*
- ✦ Butter ... *2 tbsp*

For Stuffing:

- ✦ Soya granules ... *¼ cup*
- ✦ Potatoes ... *2 no*
- ✦ Gram dal ... *½ cup*
- ✦ Sesame seeds powder ... *¼ cup*
- ✦ Green Chilies ... *4 no*
- ✦ Coriander chopped ... *¼ cup*
- ✦ Brown Onion ... *1 tbsp*
- ✦ Ginger-Garlic paste ...*1 tsp*
- ✦ Mango powder ... *1 tsp*
- ✦ Mixed Spice powder ... *1 tsp*
- ✦ Red Chili powder...*1 tsp*
- ✦ Lemon ... *1 no*
- ✦ Salt ... *to taste*

Preparation and Cooking

1. Peel and cut bottle gourd into 2 pieces and hollow the centre with a peeler, leaving ½-inch thickness around the walls. Save the pulp.

2. Rub the gourd tubes very well with lemons dipped in salt, inside out. Leave them aside for 30 minutes.
3. Meantime, soak gram dal for 30 minutes and soya granules for 15 minutes, separately.
4. Steam gourd tubes on micro High for 5 minutes. Remove and cool thoroughly.
5. Peel and cut potatoes.
6. Chop green chilies and bottle gourd pulp.
7. In a micro-safe bowl put 1 tbsp butter, potatoes, gram dal and soya meat (water drained), bottle gourd pulp and brown onion. Sprinkle 2 tbsp water; cover and cook for 6 minutes on High and stand it for 3 minutes. Slightly cool and mash.
8. Mix thoroughly the dry spices, coriander, green chilies, sesame seeds powder and salt with the mashed ingredients and check the seasoning.
9. Carefully stuff the gourd pieces (pipes).
10. Heat butter in a shallow heatproof dish for 30 seconds on High; place the stuffed gourd pieces in it one by one and roll to coat with the butter.
12. Cover the dish with cling film, pierce it with fork from one place and micro cook for 8 minutes on High. Let the dish stand for 5 minutes.
13. If you like, remove the cling film and place it under grill for 6 minutes, turning the side once.
14. With a sharp knife slice the stuffed gourd tubes into ½-inch thick slices before serving.

Serving: Garnish the dish with Tomato slices and serve at room temperature with Tomato sauce. This dish goes well with Indian and Continental meals.

Variation: Non-vegetarians may replace soya granules with 150 gm mutton mince.

Tip: This dish falls in the category of fancy cooking. With such preparation, an ordinary vegetable like gourd not only becomes extraordinary but also tasty.

6. Stuffed Peppers

Micro Cooking: 10 mins Serves: 4-6 persons

- ✦ Peppers ... *4 no medium*
- ✦ Potatoes boiled ... *1 no*
- ✦ Paneer grated ... *1 cup*
- ✦ Brown Onions ...*1 tbsp*
- ✦ Cauliflower grated ... *1 cup*
- ✦ Green Chilies chopped ... *2 no*
- ✦ Coriander chopped ... *¼ cup*
- ✦ Pomegranate seeds ... *1 tsp*
- ✦ Garam masala ... *1 tsp*
- ✦ Chili powder ... *½ tsp*
- ✦ Salt ... *to taste*
- ✦ Cheese grated ... *¼ cup*
- ✦ Oil ... *1 tbsp*

Preparation and Cooking

1. Steam cauliflower for 2 minutes on High and cool.
2. Roast pomegranate seeds for 30 seconds on High and pound to a fine powder.

3. Cut the top of the peppers and carefully hollow them; smear with a little oil and cook the empty shells on micro High for 1½ minutes. Cool slightly.
4. Grate potato and mix with paneer, steamed cauliflower and all other ingredients except cheese and oil. Mix well and check the seasoning.
5. Stuff the peppers with this mixture.
6. Divide grated cheese into 4 parts and top the peppers with it.
7. Smear the peppers with oil from outside nicely and place on the rotating table.
8. Cook on micro Medium for 7 to 8 minutes, so that cheese melts properly. Stand the dish for 2 minutes.

Note: Please keep in mind that wherever cheese is topping a dish and we want it to be melted, then cooking on Medium is advisable, otherwise the cheese will become leathery.

Serving: Serve hot with any Indian or Continental meal. Place a knife to cut the peppers into two parts as many people do not like to eat the full stuffed pepper.

Variation: Stuff the peppers with Moong Dal mixture, Soya granules or minced Meat stuffing.

7. Plain Rice

Micro Cooking: 20 mins | **Serves: 4-6 persons**

- Basmati Rice ... *2 cups*
- Water ... *1¾ cups*

Preparation and Cooking

1. Wash and soak rice for 30 to 40 minutes.
2. Mix rice and water together and cook on High for first 8 minutes, and then for next 12 minutes on Medium, covered.
3. Let the dish stand for 5 to 10 minutes.

Serving: Loosen with fork. Serve plain rice with any vegetarian or non-vegetarian Curry or Dal preparation.

Variation: Jeera Rice: Heat 2 tbsp oil on High and crackle 1 tsp cumin seeds in it. Add this oil to the rice at the end of first 8 minutes and continue cooking according to the instructions.

Tip: In microwave cooking, it is better if the rice is not stirred when being cooked. In first 8 minutes water and rice come to boiling point, so cooking on High is essential; later when the rice is absorbing the water lower heat is required, hence cooking on Medium is recommended.

8. Bhartha

Micro Cooking: 21 mins **Serves: 4-6 persons**

- Large seedless Brinjals ... *2 no*
- Brown Onions ... *¼ cup*
- Tomatoes skinned ... *4 no large*
- Ginger chopped/grated ... *2 tbsp*
- Green Chilies chopped ... *4 no*
- Green Peas boiled ... *1 cup*
- Garam masala ... *1 tsp*
- Red Chili powder ... *1 tsp/to taste*
- Coriander chopped ... *¼ cup*
- Cooking oil ... *¼ cup*
- Salt ... *to taste*

Preparation and Cooking

1. Cut each brinjal into two parts lengthwise; place them on rotating table and micro cook on High for 8 minutes; stand for 3 minutes; gently scoop out the pulp with a spoon and chop it very fine.
2. Chop skinned tomatoes.
3. Heat oil in a big micro-safe bowl on High for 1 minute and add green chilies, tomatoes and onion in it. Mix and cook on High for 4 minutes, stirring once in between.
4. Add chopped brinjal pulp, ginger, green peas, chili powder and salt to the tomato mixture; stir well; cover and cook for 5 minutes, stirring once after 3 minutes. Mash well with a wooden spoon.
5. Open the lid, sprinkle garam masala and half the coriander; cook for another 3 minutes, uncovered, so that the extra moisture evaporates.

Serving: Garnish with remaining Coriander and serve it hot with any kind of Roti/Paratha.

Tip: Bhartha stands for any preparation of well mashed and cooked vegetables/meats.

9. Vegetable Pulao/Tahri

Micro Cooking: 26 mins **Serves: 4-6 persons**

- Basmati Rice... *1½ cups*
- Cauliflower ... *½ cup*
- Carrot ... *1 no*
- Potato ... *1 no*
- Peas shelled ... *¼ cup*
- Capsicum ... *1 small*
- Ginger juliennes...*1 tbsp*
- Oil ... *3 tbsp*
- Cumin ... *1 tsp*
- Peppercorns ... *10 no*
- Cloves ... *3 no*
- Black Cardamoms ...*2 no*
- Turmeric (opt.) ... *1 tsp*
- Chili powder ... *1 tsp* (optional)
- Salt ... *2 tsp*
- Lemon juice ... *1 tbsp*
- Water/Stock ... *3¼ cups*

Preparation and Cooking

1. Wash and soak rice for 30 to 40 minutes.
2. Clean and cut all the vegetables into ½-inch pieces.

3. Steam potatoes, cauliflower, carrot and peas for 3 minutes on High and stand for 3 minutes. Add chopped capsicum.

4. Mix oil, cumin, peppercorns, cloves, black cardamoms in a big micro-safe bowl and cook on High for 3 minutes; drain rice; add to the oil and cook on High for 2 minutes, uncovered.

5. Add water, salt, turmeric, chili powder and lemon juice to the rice; cover and cook first on High for 8 minutes; uncover and add vegetables; stir gently; cover again and cook for 10 minutes more on Medium.

6. Let the dish stand for 5 to 10 minutes, and then loosen the rice with a fork before serving.

Serving: Garnish with ginger juliennes and serve with plain Curd, Papad and Pickle etc.

Variation: Cook Peas Pulao or Cauliflower Pulao the same way and garnish with Brown Onions.

Tip: This pulao is a complete meal, so it does not require many more things with it.

10. Bharvan Karela

(Stuffed Bitter Gourds)

Micro Cooking: 12 mins **Serves: 4-6 persons**

- Tender Bitter Gourds ... *6 no medium*
- Salt ... *1 tbsp*

Stuffing:

- Onion chopped ... *1 no*
- Potato mashed ... *1 cup*
- Green Chilies chopped ... *2 no*
- Mango powder ... *½ tsp*
- Mixed spice powder ... *½ tsp*
- Chili powder ... *1 tsp*
- Coriander chopped ... *¼ cup*
- Cooking oil ... *2 tbsp*
- Salt ... *to taste*

Preparation and Cooking

1. Peel and wash bitter gourds; give a slit lengthwise; take out the seeds from the centre with the help of a peeler; sprinkle salt inside and rub it nicely outside too, and keep them aside for 2 to 3 hours.

2. Wash them under tap water to remove salt; place them in the steaming basket and steam for 4 minutes on High. Let them stand for some time.

3. Meanwhile mix 1 tbsp oil, chopped onion, green chilies and tender bitter gourd seeds in a micro-safe bowl and cook on High for 3 minutes, stirring once in between.

4. Remove and mix with rest of the ingredients for the stuffing. Divide into 6 portions.

5. Stuff bitter gourds with potato mixture; smear the outer side of bitter gourd shells with remaining 1 tbsp oil; arrange them in a heatproof dish, cover with cling film and micro cook for 4 minutes on High.

6. Remove the cling film and grill the bitter gourds for 6 minutes. Stand them inside the oven for 5 minutes.

Serving: Garnish with onion rings and serve with any Indian meal.

Variation: Follow the same procedure step by step but stuff bitter gourds with any other veg or non-veg stuffing of your choice, eg. cooked minced Meat or any Dal stuffing.

Tip: The best part of this dish is that the bitter gourds are steamed and grilled, whereas commonly stuffed bitter gourds are deep or shallow fried. Hence, this is a healthy dish, not oily at all.

11. Chicken Chettinad

Micro Cooking: 20 mins **Serves: 4-6 persons**

- Chicken boneless ... *500 gm*
- Onion-Tomato paste ... *1 cup*
- Tomato puree ... *½ cup*
- Urad dal ... *2 tbsp*
- Fenugreek seeds ...*1 tbsp*
- Cloves ... *4 no*
- Cinnamon stick ... *1" piece*
- Cardamoms ... *6 no*
- Bay leaf ... *1 no*
- Curry leaves ... *1 sprig*
- Cooking oil ... *¼ cup*
- Salt ... *to taste*

For Fine Paste:

- Peppercorns ... *20 no*
- Peppercorns (optional) ... *6 no*
- Cashew nuts ... *20 no*
- Cumin ... *1 tsp*
- Turmeric ... *1 tsp*
- Poppy seeds ... *2 tsp*
- Ginger paste ... *2 tsp*
- Garlic paste ... *2 tsp*
- Fenugreek seeds ... *1 tsp*
- Red Chili whole ... *6 no*
- Lemon juice ... *2 tbsp*

Preparation and Cooking

1. Deseed the red chilies.
2. Place the dry ingredients like peppercorns, cashew nuts, cumin, poppy seeds, fenugreek seeds and whole red chilies in an envelope and roast on micro High for 1½ minutes, shaking it once in between. Remove and cool.
3. Soak urad dal.
4. Cut chicken in 1½" pieces and marinate with lemon juice, salt and ginger-garlic paste. Keep aside.
5. Grind the roasted ingredients into a fine paste with ½ cup water.
6. Heat oil in a big micro-safe bowl for 1 minute on High, add urad dal, whole spices like cardamoms, cloves, cinnamon, fenugreek seeds and curry leaves. Cook on High for 2 minutes, uncovered.

7. Add onion and tomato paste and cook on High for 2 minutes, uncovered.
8. Add tomato puree and bay leaf. Stir and cook on High for 1 minute.
9. Now mix ground masala and marinated chicken pieces. Cook on High for 2 minutes, uncovered, stirring once in between.
10. Finally, add 2 cups water; stir properly; cover the dish and cook on Medium for 10 minutes, stirring once in between. Stand the dish for 3 minutes.

Serving: Crush 6 peppercorns (optional) and sprinkle on chicken after placing it in a serving bowl.

Chicken Chettinad is a dry preparation, so serve it hot preferably with plain Dosa or Paratha. Of course, the rice eaters can relish it with plain Dal and Rice, too.

Variation: Cook Paneer or boneless Mutton with the same gravy.

For Mutton Chettinad, marinate mutton for a longer time and add 1 cup more water to the gravy while final cooking is taking place, and cook the dish on micro Medium for 13 minutes. Also give the standing time to the dish.

For Paneer Chettinad avoid step no 9; for the final cooking after adding ground masala and water cook the gravy for 6 minutes; add paneer, cover and cook only for 2 minutes. Let the dish stand for 3 minutes and serve.

Tip: Chettiyar is a place near Chennai and this exotic dish flavoured with black pepper is a speciality of the Chettiyar community.

12. Hyderabadi Fish Curry

Micro Cooking: 23 mins **Serves: 4-6 persons**

- Fish pieces ... *500 gm*
- Lemon juice ... *2 tbsp*
- Salt ... *1 tsp*
- Brown Onions ... *½ cup*
- Ginger-Garlic paste ... *1 tbsp*
- Tomato puree ... *½ cup*
- Coconut grated ... *½ no*
- Peanut powder ... *¼ cup*
- Poppy seeds ... *2 tbsp*
- Green Chilies ... *6 no*
- Curd ... *½ cup*
- Green Cardamoms ... *6 no*
- Garam masala ... *2 tsp*
- Turmeric ... *1 tsp*
- Red Chili powder ... *1 tsp*
- Cumin ... *½ tsp*
- Cooking oil ... *3 tbsp*
- Salt & Pepper ... *to taste*
- Water ... *3 cups*
- Coriander for garnishing

Preparation and Cooking

1. Soak poppy seeds in ½ cup water for 30 minutes.
2. Marinate fish pieces with lemon juice and salt.

3. Pound green cardamoms and take out the seeds.
4. Grind together brown onions, green chilies and ginger-garlic paste with ½ cup curd.
5. Grind together grated coconut and poppy seeds along with the soaking liquid.
6. Heat oil in a deep micro-safe bowl for 1 minute on High; add onion paste; stir and cook, uncovered, for 3 minutes on High.
7. Add coconut paste and peanut powder; stir well and cook uncovered, for 3 minutes on High. Uncover and add turmeric, chili powder, salt, garam masala, cardamom seeds and water to the cooked pastes.
8. Lift out the fish pieces from the marinade and place in the gravy. Cover and cook first on micro High for 6 minutes; stir once gently and then on Medium for 10 minutes.
9. Stand the dish for 5 minutes.
10. Heat 1 tsp ghee in a ladle on the gas; crackle cumin in it and pour over the cooked fish curry.

Serving: Garnish with chopped Coriander and serve it hot with steamed Rice.

Variation: Instead of fish add 6 to 8 hard-boiled Eggs (halved) in the ready gravy; cover and heat through on Reheat for 3 to 4 minutes before serving. In this case cook gravy at step 7 for 10 minutes on High, covered.

Tip: Hyderabad, in Andhra Pradesh, is known for its good and rich food as the founder rulers of the city developed many dishes according to royal tastes.

13. Grilled Fish Pomfret

Micro Cooking: 25 mins | **Serves: 4-6 persons**

✦ Pomfret/Any other fish	... *500 gm*
✦ Butter	... *1 tbsp*
✦ Salt	... *1 tsp*
✦ Pepper	... *1 tsp*
✦ Lemon juice	... *1 tbsp*
✦ Coriander chopped	... *1 cup*
✦ Green Chilies chopped	... *3 no*
✦ Ginger chopped	... *1" piece*

Preparation and Cooking

1. Wash and clean the fish. Wash again with tap or cold water and dry it on a kitchen towel. With a sharp knife cut the fish fillets in such a way from both sides that the centre bone is intact.
2. Grind together chopped coriander, green chilies, ginger and lemon juice to a fine paste. Add salt and pepper according to your taste.

3. Apply coriander paste inside the fish on both sides and rub it outside also. Keep it aside for at least 30 minutes.
4. Press the button of combination of Grill + Oven.
5. Melt butter and brush the top of the fish.
6. Place it on heatproof plate and bake for 20 to 25 minutes. After 10 minutes or so change the side and baste it with butter. When cooked from both the sides turn off the oven and leave the fish there for 5 minutes more.

Serving: Serve with Potato chips and some fresh Green Salad with any meal.

Variation: After cleaning and washing the fish, smear it only with lemon juice/vinegar and salt-pepper. Omit the green paste. Follow the same procedure.

Tip: Smearing with lemon juice or vinegar removes the fishy smell of the fish. Any fish with thicker scales should be cleaned by rubbing dry gram flour on it and then smearing it with the sour contents.

14. Meatballs in Quick Sauce

Micro Cooking: 15 mins | Serves: 4-6 persons

- Mutton mince ... *500 gm*
- Eggs ... *1 no*
- Dry Bread crumbs ... *1–1½ cups*
- Onion chopped finely ... *2 no*
- Green Chilies chopped ... *4 no*
- Ginger powder ... *1 tsp*
- Pepper powder ... *tsp*
- Mint powder ... *1 tsp*
- Coriander/Parsley chopped ... *2 tbsp*
- Salt ... *2 tsp level*

For Quick Sauce:

- Stock/Water ... *2½ cups*
- Tomato puree ... *½ cup*
- Chili-Garlic paste ... *1 tbsp*
- Butter ... *1 tbsp*
- Corn flour ... *1 tbsp*
- Ajinomoto (optional) ... *a pinch*
- Pepper powder (optional) ... *½ tsp*
- Sugar ... *1 tsp*
- Salt ... *to taste*

Preparation and Cooking

1. Mix together mutton mince, egg, salt, pepper and ginger powder in a blender (with a mincing blade attached) and churn for a few seconds.

2. Take out the mince in a separate bowl and add chopped onions, dry bread crumbs, chopped parsley/coriander and mint powder. Knead and mix well.

3. Divide the meat dough into 20-24 portions. Smear your hands with a little oil and form balls.

4. Place the meatballs in the steaming basket and cook on micro High for 8 minutes or till they are done. Let the dish stand for 5 minutes.

5. Combine stock, the water left in the steaming basket, tomato puree, chili-garlic, butter, sugar, pepper, and ajinomoto in a deep micro-safe bowl for quick sauce; cover and cook on High for 5 minutes.

6. Mix corn flour with ¼ cup water and pour in the sauce. Cover and cook for 2 minutes. Adjust salt.
7. Place meatballs in a shallow dish and pour the quick sauce over them; cover and keep aside. Reheat the dish for 2 to 3 minutes just before serving.

Serving: Garnish with Parsley or Mint and serve with boiled Rice or Pasta, or with Dinner Rolls and a good Salad.

Variation: Add 1 clove garlic and some cheese to the meat dough and make Italian Meatballs. Instead of quick sauce put them in 2 cups Tomato Sauce and serve them over Pasta.

Serve **Meatballs in Mushroom Sauce.** Cover and heat through for 2 to 3 minutes just before serving.

Meatballs can be just tossed in 2 tsp Butter, ¼ cup chopped Coriander, ¼ cup Chili-Garlic Sauce, ½ cup Tomato Sauce, and can be served as starters. For this, heat butter for 1 minute and add rest of the ingredients and cook on micro High for 1 minute, mix the meatballs, cover the dish and reheat for 2 to 3 minutes. Serve as starters in any gathering.

Serve **Meatballs in Methi Gravy.** Steam 2 cups Methi leaves for 3 minutes on High; grind with ½ cup Milk; cook the methi paste with 2 tbsp butter on High and add 1 cup Milk, ¼ cup Cream and seasoning of your choice; cover and cook for 3 minutes; add meatballs, cover and keep aside. Heat through, covered, before serving. If gravy seems dry, add ½ cup milk and adjust the salt accordingly.

Tip: Meatballs can be steamed in advance and stored under refrigeration.

15. Mushroom and Prawn Biryani

Micro Cooking: 35 mins | **Serves: 4-6 persons**

- Basmati Rice ...*1½ cups*
- Mushrooms ... *200 gm*
- Prawns ... *200 gm*
- Brown Onions ... *¾ cup*
- Tomato puree ... *¾ cup*
- Ginger-Garlic paste ... *1 tbsp*
- Turmeric powder...*1 tsp*
- Chili powder ... *1 tsp*
- Garam masala ... *1 tsp*
- Peppercorns ... *8 no*
- Green Cardamoms...*4 no*
- Bay leaf ... *1 no*
- Cinnamon ... *1" stick*
- Cloves ... *4 no*
- Cumin ... *1 tsp*
- Oil ... *¼ cup*
- Water ... *2 cups*
- Milk ... *1 cup*
- Saffron ... *a few strands*
- Green Chilies ... *4 no*
- Lemon juice ... *3 tbsp*
- Salt ... *to taste*
- Oil ... *1 tbsp*
- Coriander & Mint chopped ... *¼ cup*

Preparation and Cooking

1. Wash and soak rice for 15 minutes.
2. Boil rice in 4 cups water for 10 minutes on High with peppercorns, cardamoms, bay leaves, cinnamon and 2 tsp salt. Drain the water through a colander and place rice in an open and flatter vessel.
3. Blend ½ cup brown onion and ½ cup water.
4. Heat milk for 1 minute on Reheat, soak the saffron.
5. Wash, clean and halve the mushrooms.
6. Clean and de-vein the prawns.
7. Heat 2 tbsp oil in a large micro-safe bowl for 1 minute on High; add onion paste, tomato puree, ginger-garlic paste, turmeric and chili powder to it; and cook for 3 minutes on High, uncovered.
8. Add mushrooms, prawns and 2 cups water; sprinkle garam masala; cover with a lid and cook on High for 8 minutes. Stand the dish for 5 minutes and transfer to the other dish.
9. In the same bowl spread 1 tbsp oil; cover the base with cooked rice; sprinkle lemon juice, green chilies, fried onion, chopped coriander and mint, and spread half of mushroom-prawn mixture over it; repeat the process and top the dish with plain rice.
10. Make 2 to 3 deep holes in the rice with a finger and sprinkle saffron-soaked milk evenly.
11. Spread fried onion, coriander and mint on top.
12. Mix 1 tbsp oil and lemon juice, sprinkle on top.
13. Cover tightly with a lid or cling film and cook on High for 12 minutes. Stand the dish for 5 minutes.

Serving: Mix the pulao lightly with a fork and serve it hot with plain Curd or any Raita.

Variation: Cook Chicken Biryani in the same way. Use pieces of chicken marinated with lemon juice and salt.

16. Meatballs Pulao

Micro Cooking: 26 mins **Serves: 4-6 persons**

✦ Basmati Rice	... *1½ cups*	✦ Bay leaf	... *1 no*
✦ Meatballs	... *24 no*	✦ Cumin	... *1 tsp*
✦ Mutton stock	... *3 cups*	✦ Black Pepper powder	... *1 tsp*
✦ Tomato puree	... *¼ cup*	✦ Mint leaves	... *2 tbsp*
✦ Cocktail Onions	... *12 no*	✦ Ginger juliennes	... *1 tbsp*
✦ Lemon	... *1 no*	✦ Oil	... *3 tbsp*
✦ Peppercorns	... *10 no*	✦ Salt	... *to taste*
✦ Garam masala	... *1 tsp*		

Preparation and Cooking

1. Wash and soak rice for 30 minutes.
2. Heat oil in a large micro-safe bowl for 1 minute on High; add cumin and peppercorns and cook for 1 minute on High; add bay leaf and rice and cook for 2 minutes on High; add mutton stock,

lemon juice and rest of the spices; cover and cook on High for 7 minutes.

3. Open the lid; stir rice gently; mix meatballs, cocktail onions, salt and half the mint leaves; cover again and cook on Medium for 15 minutes. Stand the dish for 5 minutes.

4. Loosen the rice with a fork before serving.

Serving: Garnish with Ginger juliennes and remaining Mint leaves and serve it hot with Cucumber Raita.

Tip: This dish finds reference in our great epic the 'Mahabharata'. According to food history, this was a favourite dish of Duryodhana and it was called 'Pishthaudana' that means a rice dish cooked with ground meat patties or balls.

Note: The recipe of meatballs is given in 'Meatballs in Quick Sauce'.

17. Chicken Tikka Tandoori Style

Micro Cooking: 10 mins **Serves: 4-6 persons**

- Chicken ... *800 gm*
  Or
- Chicken breast...*600 gm*
- Hung Curd ... *2 cup*
- Ginger-Garlic paste ... *1 tbsp*
- Red Chili powder ... *1 tbsp*
- Salt ... *2 tsp*
- Cumin powder ... *1 tsp*
- Coriander powder...*1 tsp*
- Ginger powder ... *1 tsp*
- Pepper powder ... *1 tsp*
- Garam masala ... *1 tsp*
- Red Tandoori colour ... *½ tsp*

Preparation and Cooking

1. Wash and cut chicken into 12 pieces or cut boneless chicken into 1½-inch pieces.
2. Mix all the dry ingredients with hung curd and rub on the chicken pieces. Thus marinate chicken and keep aside for 2 to 3 hours.

3. Arrange the marinated chicken pieces on the outer side of a micro-safe platter and cook on micro High for first 6 minutes and then on micro Medium for next 4 to 5 minutes.
4. Take them out and check the doneness of chicken. If done, serve them hot. Boneless chicken pieces will be cooked within 6 to 7 minutes.

Serving: Serve the Tikkas on a platter of fresh Salad with green Chutney and Onion rings as starters.

Variation: Add Mint powder or Kasoori Methi to the curd marinade before marinating the chicken pieces.

Cut Paneer into 2" cubes and marinate in the same curd mixture and bake in the same manner in a hot oven for 15 to 20 minutes.

Tip: To get Hung Curd, put 3 cups of curd in a muslin cloth, tie it and keep in a sieve, or hang it with something for 2 hours. Use as required.

Note: Don't throw the nourishing Whey; collect it; chill it and consume it as a refreshing drink. You may flavour it with Salt and Pepper or Rooh Afza, etc.

18. Stuffed and Baked Cauliflower

Micro Cooking: 16 mins **Serves: 4-6 persons**

- Cauliflower medium sized ... *1 head*
- Onion-Tomato paste ... *1 cup*
- Ginger-Garlic paste ... *1 tbsp*
- Almond/Cashew nut paste ... *¼ cup*
- Fresh Cream ... *1 tbsp*
- Mixed Spice powder ... *1 tsp*
- Red Chili powder ... *1 tsp*
- Oregano ... *1 tsp*
- Lemon juice ... *1 tsp*
- Cheese grated ... *¼ cup*
- Salt ... *to taste*

Preparation and Cooking

1. Wash cauliflower and soak it in enough water having 1 tsp salt and 1 tsp lemon juice for 30 minutes to 1 hour, so that it gets cleaned thoroughly.
2. Take it out and place it in steaming basket with ¼ cup water underneath and cook on micro High

for 6 minutes, covered. Remove from oven and cover to keep it warm.

3. In a separate bowl mix all other ingredients except cheese. Check the salt and pepper.
4. Take out the cauliflower; with a butter knife gently open the flowerets and apply the mixture all over inside and outside the flowerets; cover it properly with masala.
5. Place the cauliflower in a micro-safe plate or a shallow dish and sprinkle grated cheese all over it.
6. Bake on Combination-1 mode for 10 minutes. Cauliflower will be heated through properly, cheese will melt and top will appear golden brown.
7. Stand it for 3 minutes inside the oven itself.

Serving: Surround with Tomato slices or Cucumber wedges, or garnish the way you like, and serve it hot with any Indian or Continental meal.

Place a knife and fork with it for cutting the desired size pieces.

Variation: Stuff cauliflower with well flavoured 1 cup Spinach puree mixed with ½ cup Cheese Sauce and ¼ cup Cheese sprinkled all over it. Garnish it with Tomato wedges.

Tip: Boil cauliflower in advance; apply stuffing mixture; top with grated cheese; cut the garnishing and store everything under refrigeration; take it out 1 hour before preparing for the meal and bake just before serving.

Note: If your microwave does not have Combination mode, you can bake this dish in Convection mode, but preheat it before use.

19. Shepherd's Pie

Micro Cooking: 35-40 mins **Serves: 4-6 persons**

- Mutton mince... *500 gm*
- Potatoes ... *500 gm*
- Butter ... *2 tbsp*
- Onion chopped ... *1 no*
- Tomato puree ... *½ cup*
- Corn flour ... *1 tbsp*
- Water/Stock ... *1 cup*
- Pepper powder ... *1 tsp*
- Milk ... *⅓ cup*
- Mint powder ... *1tsp*
- Ginger powder ... *1 tsp*
- Salt ... *to taste*

Preparation and Cooking

1. Peel and wash potatoes; halve them and place in the steaming basket: microwave on High for 7 minutes and stand for 5 minutes.
2. Remove and mash them immediately because potatoes are handled best when still hot. Mix with milk and ½ tsp salt; knead well and keep aside.

3. Melt half the butter, add chopped onion and cook on micro High for 2 minutes.
4. Remove and add minced meat and salt; stir well and cook on micro High for 3 minutes uncovered, stirring once in between.
5. Loosen it with the fork; add water/stock, tomato puree, pepper, ginger and mint powders and cook covered on micro High for 3 minutes.
6. Meantime mix corn flour with 3 tbsp water. Pour it into the meat sauce, stir well, cover and cook on High for 2 minutes. Let the dish stand for 5 minutes. Check the seasoning.
7. Smear a micro-safe square/rectangular glass dish with cooking oil and put the meat sauce in it, spreading it evenly.
8. Layer the mashed potatoes over the meat covering it fully.
9. Make a rough surface with the fork on top of the potatoes; dot the pie with rest of the butter and bake it in Combination-1 mode for 20 to 25 minutes; or bake it in preheated Convection mode (conventional oven) for 35 to 40 minutes.

Serving: Serve it hot with crisp Garlic Bread and a light Soup.

Variation: Use 2 cups finely chopped mixed Vegetables instead of the meat and follow rest of the recipe. Add 1 tsp mixed spice powder too.

Tip: Always handle potatoes when still hot but use them when cold. That's why potatoes are first peeled and then boiled here in the recipe.

Note: We have photographed a vegetarian variation here.

20. Tomatoes Rellenos

(Stuffed Tomatoes)

Micro Cooking: 15 mins **Serves: 4-6 persons**

- Tomatoes ... *6 no large*
- Mixed vegetables chopped ... *1 cup*
  Or
- Mushroom chopped ... *1 cup*
- Onion finely chopped ... *1 no*
- Ginger grated ... *2 tbsp*
- Green Chilies ... *3 no*
- Pepper powder ... *1 tsp*
- Parsley chopped ...*2 tbsp*
- Boiled Rice ... *1 cup*
- Cheese grated ... *¼ cup*
- Bread slices ... *2 no large*
- Oil ... *3 tbsp*
- Mixed Spice powder ... *1 tsp*
- Butter ... *1 tbsp*
- Salt ... *to taste*

Preparation and Cooking

1. Wash and dry tomatoes. Take out a slice from the stem side and scoop the pulp carefully with a peeler or a small teaspoon without breaking the tomato shells. Keep the pulp aside.

2. Now sprinkle inside of tomatoes with salt generously and invert them over a wire mesh kept in a plate for 1 hour at least so that all the water drains out and the tomato shells are dry and ready to be filled. Moisture in tomato shells breaks them while baking.
3. Deseed and chop green chilies. Keep aside.
4. Boil mixed vegetables with 2 tbsp water and ¼ tsp salt on High for 3 minutes, covered.
5. Heat oil in a micro-safe bowl for 1 minute, add cumin and cook on High for 1 minute.
6. Remove and add chopped onion and green chilies in it and cook on High for 2 minutes, uncovered. Add tomato pulp and ginger; cook for 2 minutes on High, uncovered; and finally mix rice, cooked vegetables, cheese, parsley, salt and dry spices. Stir properly. Slightly cool the stuffing. If you are using mushroom, then cook them along with tomato pulp.
7. Place bread slices in an electric grinder and make fresh breadcrumbs.
8. Cook the empty shells of tomatoes on micro High for 1 minute.
9. Brush them with a little oil from outside and stuff them with the rice-vegetable-tomato pulp stuffing; sprinkle the top with breadcrumbs and dot with butter.
10. Cook on micro Medium for 5 minutes. Stand the dish for 3 minutes and serve.

You may cover stuffed tomatoes with cling film and cook on High for 8 to 10 minutes for softer shells.

Serving: Serve hot with any Indian or Continental meal.

Variation: Instead of boiled rice use boiled Noodles and Vegetables.

Instead of vegetables, use leftover shredded Chicken/ minced Meat for stuffing.

Use Paneer and vegetable combination for stuffing.

21. Buttered Broccoli, Mushrooms and Peppers

Micro Cooking: 17 mins **Serves: 4-6 persons**

- Broccoli flowerets ... *2 cups*
- Mushrooms halved ... *2 cups*
- Red pepper ... *1 no small*
- Green pepper ... *1 no small*
- Butter ... *2 tbsp*
- Yellow pepper ... *1 no small*
- Garlic minced ... *1 tbsp*
- Lemon juice ... *1 tbsp*
- Sesame seeds ... *2 tbsp*
- Salt ... *to taste*
- Freshly crushed Peppercorns ... *1 tbsp*

Preparation and Cooking

1. Wash broccoli in enough water; sprinkle 1 tsp salt; mix and place in steaming basket or in a dish with a lid and cook for 5 minutes on micro High.

2. Place sesame seeds in an envelope and roast on micro High for 2 minutes, shaking once in between.
3. Wash, clean and cut peppers in matchstick fashion.
4. Heat butter in a micro-safe shallow dish for 1 minute on High; add minced garlic, 1 tsp salt and crushed pepper; cook on High for 2 minutes, stirring once.
5. Add halved mushrooms and cook on High for 2 minutes, uncovered.
6. Add broccoli, peppers and lemon juice; stir properly, so that the vegetables are coated well with garlic and butter; cover with a lid and cook for 5 minutes, so that broccoli, too, absorbs garlic-butter aroma. Stand the dish for 2 minutes.
7. Mix the vegetables well but with a light hand and sprinkle with toasted sesame seeds.

Serving: Serve it hot along with any non-vegetarian dish and Dal-Rice meal. Tastes good with plain Parathas also.

Tip: Always roast at least ½ cup sesame seeds. Use as much as required and the rest can be stored in a dry bottle for future use.

22. Momos

Micro Cooking: 6 mins **Serves: 4-6 persons**

- Flour ... *100 gm*
- Olive oil ... *1 tsp*
- Egg yolk ... *1 no*
- Salt ... *a pinch*
- Veg or non-veg well flavoured stuffing ... *1 cup*

Preparation and Cooking

1. Combine flour, oil, egg yolk and salt and make dough; keep it covered for 2 hours and use.
2. Divide into three parts. Roll one part into a thin square shaped chapati and cut into 4 equal portions.
3. Place 2 tsp filling in 1 portion; hold all the 4 corners and carefully give a twist to seal momo; in this way finish stuffing all the 4 portions. Repeat the process with the second and third parts.

4. Place all the momos in a steaming basket with ¼ cup water underneath and steam on micro Medium for 6 minutes. Let the dish stand for 5 minutes.

Serving: Serve warm or at room temperature with Szechuan sauce or Tomato sauce. You may serve a cup of clear veg or non-veg Soup, too, along with it, so that you can enjoy the taste of tangy-hot Szechuan sauce.

Variation: If you want to cook Momos without Eggs, take 200gm Maida + a pinch each of Baking powder and Salt. Mix with water into a smooth dough and leave it overnight. Follow the steps given above using any vegetarian filling of your choice. Steam in the traditional way for 10 minutes.

Tip: Momos is becoming a popular snack that is available at selected outlets.

23. Chinese Fried Rice

Micro Cooking: 11 mins Serves: 4-6 persons

- Rice parboiled ...2 *cups*
- Vegetables parboiled ... 2 *cups*
- Eggs ... 3 *no*
- Onion chopped ... 1 *no*
- Cooking oil/ Chili oil ... 3 *tbsp*
- Soy sauce ... 1 *tbsp*
- Salt ... 1 *tsp*

Preparation and Cooking

1. Heat oil in a large micro-safe bowl for 1 minute on High; add chopped onion and cook on High for 1 minute.

2. Add beaten eggs, and ½ tsp salt to the oil; cook for 2 minutes on Medium, stirring once.

3. Mix boiled vegetables with the egg mixture and cook on Medium for 3 minutes, stirring once.

4. Add rice and salt; sprinkle soy sauce and stir gently; sprinkle 2 tbsp water or stock; cover the dish with a lid and Reheat for 5 minutes so that the rice is very hot.

Serving: Serve with any of the Chinese dishes.

Variation: Instead of vegetables, use cooked and chopped Chicken or Shrimps.

Note: If you have to parboil rice in the microwave, put 1 cup raw rice and 5 cups water in a large bowl; boil for 13 minutes on High; drain the water immediately through a colander and place rice under the tap water. Drain well and use. Fried rice comes out very well if parboiled rice is cooked in advance and kept under refrigeration for some time.

Tip: In Chinese food, great care is taken to provide contrasting flavours, textures both crunchy and soft, and a pleasing variety of colour and shapes (in which vegetables play an important role). That is why the Chinese dishes are not only visually appealing but also satisfying to the appetite. A small quantity of meats added to their dishes make an ordinary food item an extraordinary one, hence you find meats and vegetables combined in these dishes. Nutritionally, these dishes are excellent because whatever method of cooking is used, the food ingredients are cooked quickly, so they retain their natural goodness.

Vegetarian concept has come to us because India is largely a vegetarian country, so we keep converting the recipes to suit us.

24. Chili Chicken with Chili Garlic Sauce

Micro Cooking: 12 mins | Serves: 4-6 persons

- Chicken breast ... *1*
- Chili sauce ... *1 tsp*
- Soy sauce ... *1 tsp*
- Worcestershire sauce ... *1 tsp*
- Salt ... *1 tsp*
- Vinegar ... *2 tbsp*
- Chili-Garlic sauce ... *1 tbsp*
- Tomato sauce ... *1 tbsp*
- Garlic finely chopped ... *1 tbsp*
- Corn flour ... *3 tbsp*
- Capsicum cut into roundels ... *1 no*
- Ajinomoto ... *a pinch*
- Chicken stock... *1½ cups*
- Oil ... *3 tbsp*

Preparation and Cooking

1. Debone and cut the chicken into 1" pieces. Marinate with vinegar, chili sauce, soy sauce, salt, ajinomoto and Worcestershire sauce for 2 hours.
2. Strain and save the liquid.

3. Sprinkle 2 tbsp corn flour over the chicken pieces and mix well.
4. Place chicken pieces in a shallow micro-safe dish; pour oil over them and mix with your hand. Cook on High for 4 minutes, stirring once. Cover and stand it for 3 minutes.
5. In another bowl add oil, chopped garlic and capsicum rings, mix and cook on High for 2 minutes, uncovered; take out the capsicum pieces and keep for garnishing.
6. In the same bowl combine 1 cup stock, liquid from the chicken marinade, tomato sauce and chili garlic sauce, and cook on High for 3 minutes, stirring once after 2 minutes. Mix corn flour with ½ cup stock; pour in the hot sauce; mix well and cook for 1 minute on High.
7. Check the seasoning; pour this sauce over cooked chicken; stir well; cover and cook on micro High for 6 minutes.

Serving: Garnish Chili chicken with capsicum rings and serve hot with Rice/Noodles.

25. Chinese Sweet-n-Sour Vegetables

Micro Cooking: 15 mins | Serves: 4-6 persons

- White vinegar ... *1 cup*
- Tomato sauce... *½-¾ cup*
- Garlic paste ... *2 tsp*
- Sugar ... *¼ cup*
- Red Chili powder ... *1 tbsp*
- Onion ... *1 no*
- Tomato ... *1 no large*
- Chili oil ... *2 tbsp*
- Corn flour ... *2 tbsp*
- Water ... *1½ cups*
- Ajinomoto ... *a pinch*
- Salt ...*1 tbsp*
- Cauliflower flowerets ...*1 cup*
- Capsicum cubed...*½ cup*
- Carrot cubes ... *½ cup*
- Beans chopped ...*¼ cup*
- Mushrooms halved (opt.) ...*½ cup*
- Egg white (opt.) ...*1 no*

Preparation and Cooking

1. Chop onion and tomato into 1" square pieces.
2. Heat oil in a micro-safe bowl for 1 minute on High; add onion and cook on High for 1 minute; add

garlic paste and cook on High for 1 minute; add vinegar, 1 cup water, tomato sauce, chili powder, sugar, salt and ajinimoto; mix it and cook on High for 6 minutes or till sugar is fully dissolved, stirring once.

3. Mix corn flour with ½ cup water and pour into boiling sauce; stir well and cook for 3 minutes, stirring once. Beat egg white very stiff and mix with the sauce for the shine.

4. Take it out; add chopped tomato and capsicum and keep it covered to avoid any formation of film on top of the sauce.

5. Steam the chopped vegetables in the steaming basket for 3 minutes on High. Stand them for 3 minutes and then add them to the sauce.

Serving: Serve with Fried Rice/Noodles.

Variation: Add cooked Chicken/Prawns/Pork or Mutton to this sauce.

Cut 250 gm boneless meat of your choice into small pieces or thin slices and marinate with 1 cup vinegar, a pinch of ajinomoto, salt, pepper, chili and mustard powders and 1 tbsp oil for 2 hours; strain the liquid and save; sprinkle ¼ cup flour and 1 tsp salt; add a dash of tomato and chili sauce, mix well and place in a micro-safe bowl (in which 2 tbsp oil has been added) and cook on High for 6 to 8 minutes. Add the saved marinade to the meat and place it in the sweet-n-sour sauce with vegetables or without them. Cover and cook for 2 minutes on High and serve.

Note: Chicken and prawns will be nicely cooked this way but if you are using mutton/pork then it is advisable to fry the meat after adding flour and 1 egg to it.

26. Pasta with Meat and Italian Tomato Sauce

(Pasta with Bolognese Sauce)

Micro Cooking: 35 mins **Serves: 4-6 persons**

- Spaghetti boiled...*3 cups*
- Cheese grated ... *¼ cup*

For Italian Tomato Sauce:

- Tomatoes ... *1000 gm*
- Olive oil/Butter...*2 tbsp*
- Pepper ... *1 tsp*
- Chili powder ... *1 tsp*
- Red Pepper flakes...*½ tsp*
- Italian herbs ... *1 tsp*
- Salt ... *to taste*
- Garlic minced ... *1 tbsp*
- Mutton mince...*300 gm*
- Mushroom chopped (opt.) ...*6 no*

Preparation and Cooking

1. Place tomatoes in a blender and puree.
2. Strain through a rice colander so that seeds are separated.

3. In a big micro-safe bowl heat butter for 30 seconds on High and add minced garlic; cook for 1 minute on High and mix minced mutton; cook for 3 minutes on High, stirring once and take it out.

4. In the same bowl combine all other ingredients for Italian sauce except oregano.

5. Cook uncovered on High for 15 minutes, stirring thrice.

6. Add mutton mince and oregano to the tomato sauce and cook it covered for 5 minutes more on High, stirring once in between. Let the sauce stand for 5 minutes before using it.

7. Sprinkle oregano and chopped parsley or basil.

Assembly: In a square or round micro-safe dish put 1 tsp oil and spread it properly.

Cover the base with boiled spaghetti; pour hot tomato-meat sauce over it and sprinkle with grated cheese.

Cook on Combination mode for 8 to 10 minutes. Press Combi-1; set the time and start. The dish can also be baked in Convection mode for 30 minutes.

Serving: Serve hot pasta as a main dish with any Continental meal or with Spinach and Mushroom Soup.

Variation: Cook Italian Tomato Sauce without Mutton mince but add mixed Italian herbs available in leading stores.

27. Lasagna

Micro Cooking: 36 mins **Serves: 4-6 persons**

- Tomato-Meat sauce ... *3 cups*
- Cheese sauce ... *1 recipe*
- Grated Parmesan cheese ... *½ cup*
- Lasagna sheets ... *6 to 8 sheets*
- Oil ... *1 tbsp*
- Large Rectangular/ Square micro safe dish

Preparation and Cooking

1. Boil 4 cups water in a square dish for 6 minutes on High; drop in the lasagna sheets and pour oil; cook on High for 10 minutes; drain the water and rinse pasta with tap water. Keep them warm.
2. Grease a micro-safe dish and spread half of the tomato-meat sauce evenly to cover the base.
3. Cover it with boiled lasagna sheets.

4. Spread cheese sauce over it and sprinkle a little grated cheese, too.

5. Repeat the process one more time and sprinkle grated cheese on top.

6. Cook on micro Medium for 20 minutes or till cheese is melted and the sauce is bubbling; or bake in moderately hot oven for 35 to 40 minutes.

Note: The recipe of Tomato-meat sauce has been given in 'Pasta in Italian Meat Sauce'.

Serving: Serve it hot with Italian meal or any other Continental meal.

Variation: Cook Vegetarian Lasagna: Take 2 cups spinach puree + ½ cup tomato puree + 2 tsp Ginger-garlic paste + 1 tsp Italian herbs + 2 tbsp brown Onion + 1 tbsp Butter + 1 tsp Chili-garlic, Salt and Pepper to taste. Mix all the ingredients together and add ½ cup Cream/ Malai. Use it in place of meat sauce.

Tip: You can make your own lasagna sheets with the basic noodle dough; roll the dough into very thin rectangular sheets and cut them into desired size of your baking dish.

Basic Noodle Dough: Knead together 100gm white Flour + 1 tsp Olive oil + 1 Egg yolk + 1 pinch of Salt. Keep it covered for 2 hours and use as required.

I personally like to cook Lasagna with pancakes that are very light and make an excellent dish. Since these days all kind of ready pasta is available, and working ladies have less time at hand to plan the meals and the party menus, this simple recipe given here can be very handy.

Note: If you have limited time at hand, boil lasagna sheets on top of the gas stove the way we boil Macaroni or Spaghetti simultaneously making other sauces, etc. This will reduce the micro cooking time, too.

28. Paella

(Saffron-flavoured Chicken Rice)

Micro Cooking: 33 mins **Serves: 4-6 persons**

- Rice ... *2 cups*
- Chicken ... *1 no*
- Fish chunks ... *1 cup*
- French Beans chopped ... *½ cup*
- Green Peas shelled ... *½ cup*
- Tomato puree ... *½ cup*
- Onion sliced ... *1 no*
- Garlic chopped ...*3 tbsp*
- Bay leaf ... *1 no*
- Saffron ... *a big pinch*
- Cooking oil ... *3 tbsp*
- Chicken stock ... *4 cups*
- Pepper powder ... *2 tsp*
- Salt ... *to taste*

Preparation and Cooking

1. Clean and cut chicken into 8 pieces.
2. Soak rice for 30 minutes to 1 hour.
3. Heat oil in a micro-safe bowl for 1 minute on High; add sliced onion and chopped garlic; stir well and cook, uncovered for 2 minutes on High.
4. Add cut chicken pieces; turn to coat well with oil and cook for 8 minutes on High, covered, turning the chicken pieces once after 5 minutes.
5. Add rice, green peas, beans, fish chunks and saffron; mix well and cook for 2 minutes, uncovered.
6. Add stock, salt, pepper and bay leaf. Cover with a lid and cook for 20 minutes, first 6 minutes on High and next 14 minutes on Medium, stirring once after 6 minutes. Let the dish stand for 5 minutes.

Serving: Serve immediately before rice becomes too dry.

Tip: Paella is an Italian style Saffron-flavoured Rice Pulao. Unlike Indian dishes, this is a mildly flavoured rice dish.

29. Pizza

(Italian Bread)

Micro Cooking: 6 mins   Baking: 10 mins. per pizza

- Pizza shells ... *4 no*
- Mushrooms sliced ...*1 cup*
- Capsicums thinly sliced ... *½ cup*
- Tomato wedges from ... *1 tomato*
- Olives/Baby Corns halved ... *12 no*
- Mozzarella Cheese grated ... *1½ cups*
- Pizza sauce ... *1½ cups*

For Pizza Sauce:

- Onion-Tomato paste ... *1 cup*
- Tomato puree ... *1 cup*
- Chili-Garlic sauce ... *1 tbsp*
- Butter ... *1 tsp*
- Oregano ... *2 tsp*
- Pepper powder ... *2 tsp*
- Ajwain ... *1 tsp*
- Sugar ... *1 tsp*
- Capsicum finely chopped ... *¼ cup*
- Chili powder ... 1 tsp (optional)
- Parsley chopped ...*2 tbsp*
- Bay leaf ... *1 no*
- Salt ... *to taste*

Preparation and Cooking

1. Heat butter in a micro-safe bowl for 1 minute on High and add ajwain (carom seeds). Cook on High for 1 minute, remove and add chopped capsicum and cook again for 1 minute on High.
2. Now add all the other ingredients for pizza sauce to it except parsley. Mix well and cover with the lid. Cook on micro High for 3 minutes and remove the dish. Take out the bay leaf and sprinkle parsley.
3. Preheat the Convection mode of your microwave oven for 15 minutes at 200° Celsius.

Assembly: Apply pizza sauce generously on pizza shells. Sprinkle some cheese over them; arrange sliced vegetables or meats and finally top with grated cheese. Cover nicely from all sides.

Baking: Bake pizzas in hot oven one by one for 10 minutes or till cheese melts.

Serving: Cut into wedges and serve hot with Mustard/ Tomato Sauce as a starter or with Soup, Salad and any of the Italian or Continental baked dishes.

Variation: You may even top the pizza with shredded chicken, chopped pineapple and boiled corn.

Tip: If your microwave has no Convection mode, then first crisp one side of the pizza shell under the grill for 2 to 3 minutes, then apply pizza sauce and veggies/ meats and grill for 5 minutes or till cheese melts. Repeat with rest of the shells.

Note: Prepared Pizza can be reheated very well in the micro mode. Place 1 full pizza of room temperature on a paper plate or kitchen paper towel and reheat on High for 1½ to 2 minutes.

Avoid: Having too much of pizzas without salad or soups is bad for health because the food value of this so-called fast food is poor!

Enjoy junk food as a mini meal and cultivate a habit of having nutritious soups and salads because a healthy diet should include fibrous food like vegetables, fruits and dry fruits along with other food items.

Special note:

Bake your own Pizza shells—

Sieve 250 gm Flour and 1 tsp Salt together in a bowl and keep in a warm place. Mix 1 tsp dry Yeast and 2 tsp Sugar in 4 tbsp warm Milk and stir till creamy. Rub 2 tbsp Butter into the flour and mix creamy yeast with it. Beat 1 Egg and stir in the flour. Now knead the flour thoroughly; cover it and put in a warm place until double in size. Preheat the oven. Knead the flour once again for 2-3 minutes continuously and roll into large flattened circles about ½-inch thick and 6-inch in diameter or roll small cocktail pizzas. Prick the surface with a fork. Arrange in a baking tray and bake in the preheated Moderately Hot micro oven for 15 to 20 minutes. Remove, cool and store.

Cakes and Desserts

Desserts, generally served at the end of any meal, are the epitome of good taste and quality of food. Desserts included in this section are the ones that can be selected for any Indian, Continental, Chinese or Italian food. The simplest methods of cooking are adopted for the ease in preparing them. Cakes can be converted into desserts if served in a suggested method with recommended sauces, and as such, can also be served at tea or high tea.

1. Sevian

(Sweet Vermicelli)

Micro Cooking: 15 mins **Serves: 4-6 persons**

- Vermicelli ... *1 cup*
- Sugar ... *½ cup*
- Ghee ... *2 tbsp*
- Water ... *1 cup*
- Saffron ... *a few strands*
- Cardamom powder ... *½ tsp*
- Nuts chopped ...*2-3 tbsp*

Preparation and Cooking

1. Soak saffron in 2 tbsp warm water.
2. Mix sugar and water and boil on High for 3 minutes.
3. Add saffron and cardamom powder in sugar syrup.
4. Heat ghee in a micro-safe bowl for 2 minutes on High; add vermicelli; stir and cook on High for 2 minutes, uncovered, stirring once.
5. Add sugar syrup to the vermicelli; stir well; cover and cook for 5 minutes. Stand the dish for 5 minutes.

Serving: Loosen vermicelli lightly with a fork; garnish with chopped nuts and serve dry at room temperature as a dessert or breakfast dish.

Variation: **Sheer Khurma:** Add 1 tbsp more Ghee + ¼ cup more Sugar + 2½ cups Milk + 5 dry Dates washed, soaked and chopped + 1 tbsp Chironji fried in ghee. At step no 5 of cooking, add milk and dates and boil for 13 to 15 minutes on Medium. Garnish with chironji and serve it hot.

Tip: Dry sweet vermicelli or with milk called Sukhi Sevian and Sevian ki Kheer respectively become special on the occasion of Id-ul-Milad when Muslim families prepare and serve it to their near and dear ones.

2. Eggless Cake

Micro Cooking: 6-8 mins **Serves: 4-6 persons**

- Flour ... *150 gm*
- Butter ... *100 gm*
- Milkmaid (condensed milk) ... *200 gm*
- Baking powder ... *1 tsp*
- Baking soda ... *½ tsp*
- Vanilla essence ... *1 tsp*
- Medium sized micro-safe glass dish or a ring mould.

Preparation and Cooking

1. Sieve flour, baking powder and baking soda together.
2. Beat butter and Milkmaid. Add rest of the ingredients and mix well. Add ½ cup water to make a batter of dropping consistency.
3. Put in a mould, bake on Combi-2/3 for 6–8 minutes; remove, check by inserting a knitting needle in it.
4. Let it stand for 5 to 10 minutes or till the cake cools down. Cut the cake and serve.

Variation: For Eggless Chocolate Cake: Reduce 2 tbsp flour and add 2 tbsp level Coco powder + 1 tbsp powdered Sugar and follow the same procedure.

3. Grandma's Gud Ke Chawal

Micro Cooking: 30 mins **Serves: 4-6 persons**

✦ Basmati Rice	... *1½ cups*	✦ Cinnamon	... *2" stick*
✦ Ghee	... *3 tbsp melted*	✦ Ginger powder	... *¼ tsp*
✦ Gud (jaggery)	...*200 gm*	✦ Raisins	... *¼ cup*
✦ Cloves	... *6 no*	✦ Nuts chopped	... *2 tbsp*
✦ Cardamoms	... *3 no*	✦ Water	... *1 cup*

Preparation and Cooking

1. Wash and soak rice for 1 hour.
2. Coarsely pound cloves, cardamoms and cinnamon together. Clean and soak raisins.
3. Break jaggery into small pieces and place in a micro-safe bowl with ¼ cup water and cook for 2 minutes on High or till it is melted.
4. In a big micro-safe bowl heat ghee for 1 minute on High; add pounded spices to it and cook for 1 minute on High.
5. Add rice and stir well; put water; cover the dish and cook for 5 minutes on High; stir well; add gur mixture and ½ cup water; cover with a lid and cook on Medium for 15 minutes; stir in the raisins and half the chopped nuts and cook again for 5 minutes on Medium. Stand the dish for 10 minutes.

Serving: Garnish with rest of the nuts and serve warm.

Tip: This traditional special dish from North India is becoming rare day by day. It seems very simple but is quite tricky if cooked traditionally. But it is very easy now to cook it in microwave, as neither does it stick to the bottom nor burn.

It was a favourite dish of my ma-in-law; she had mastery over it but spent the whole day in the kitchen to cook it for her grandchildren.

4. Hot Milk Sponge Cake

Micro Baking: 45 mins **Serves: 4-6 persons**

✦ Flour	... *1 cup*	✦ Sugar	... *1 cup*
✦ Baking powder	... *1 tsp*	✦ Lemon juice	... *2 tsp*
✦ Salt	... *a pinch*	✦ Milk	... *¼ cup+ 2 tbsp*
✦ Eggs	... *3 no*	✦ Butter	... *1 tsp*

Preparation and Cooking

1. Preheat Convection mode at 180° Celsius.
2. Sift together flour, baking powder and salt twice.
3. Beat eggs until light and foamy. Beating constantly gradually add sugar, lemon juice and flour mixture.
4. Heat milk and butter for 30 seconds on Reheat.
5. Quickly add to egg mixture, stir until smooth.
6. Pour into a 9-inch un-greased loaf tin. Bake in moderately hot oven for 45 minutes. Remove; invert on wire rack until cake is cold. Unmould the cake.

Serving: Use sponge cake for covering with icing or for trifle puddings, etc.

5. Almond Chikki

(Almond Brittle)

Micro Cooking: 7-8 mins **Serves: 4-6 persons**

✦ Sugar	... *½ cup*	✦ Almonds coarsely powdered	... *¼ cup*
✦ Butter	... *1 tsp*		
✦ Water	... *¼ cup*		

Preparation and Cooking

1. Grease a plate and keep aside.
2. In a medium sized micro-safe bowl combine butter, sugar and water and cook on High for 7 minutes, stirring twice in between.
3. Add powdered almonds when the sugar is melted and caramelised.
4. Pour into the greased plate and spread it with a flat knife. Let it set and cool for some time; mark with a knife; break into pieces and store in an airtight jar.

Alternative: Clean and grease a small area of your working platform; pour the caramelised sugar on it; wait for a few seconds; roll it with a rolling pin as thin as you can; mark the squares with a butter knife and cool the almond brittle. Break it into pieces and store.

Serving: Serve it after meals or enjoy any time during winters.

Variation: Add roasted Peanuts or Cashew nuts in the same proportion to the caramelized sugar and follow the process.

Add mixed nuts to the caramelized sugar.

6. Apple Custard Meringue

Micro Cooking: 18 mins **Serves: 4-6 persons**

✦ Apples ... *3 no medium*	✦ Sugar ... *4 tbsp*
✦ Eggs ... *2 no*	✦ Custard powder... *1 tbsp*
✦ Milk ... *2 cups*	✦ Vanilla essence ... *½ tsp*
✦ Lemon juice ... *1 tbsp + 1 tsp*	✦ Fresh Cream ... *½ cup*
	✦ Sugar ... *1 tbsp*

Preparation and Cooking

1. Powder sugar in an electric mixer.
2. Wash, peel and cut apples into small pieces and mix with lemon juice. Put them in a micro-safe bowl, add ¼ cup water, cover with a lid and cook for 4 minutes on High to stew them.
3. Let them stand for 5 minutes, remove and mash with a wooden spoon when still hot.

4. Add 2 tbsp powdered sugar and keep aside.
5. Heat milk for 1 minute on High.
6. Separate egg yolks and whites.
7. Mix egg yolks, sugar and custard powder in a micro-safe bowl and beat with the egg beater; add 1¾ cups heated milk and whisk again to a smooth mixture. Cook for 3 minutes on micro High, stirring twice with the whisk every 1 minute, so that no lumps are formed and egg custard is smooth.
8. Remove and add half the essence in the custard.
9. Beat cream and mix with 1 tbsp powdered sugar and 1 tsp lemon juice.
10. In an 8-inch micro-safe bowl, first place a layer of stewed apples, then gently spread the layer of egg custard and in the end put cream over the custard.
11. Beat the egg whites very stiff and mix 2 tbsp powdered sugar and rest of the essence. Now cover the top of the dish with the beaten eggs.
12. Cook on Combi-1 for 10 minutes. The meringue should be just golden brown. Serve the dish hot.

Note: If you prefer the dish cold, you may just put the dish under the grill only for the specified period.

Serving: Serve hot or cold as a dessert with any meal.

Variation: Use stewed Guavas instead of apples, rest follow the same process. You may stew the guavas and pass through a sieve, as many people do not like the seeds.

Tip: Meringue is defined as stiffly beaten and flavoured egg whites cooked in oven or in a liquid.

7. Coconut Caramel Steamed Pudding

Micro Cooking: 24 mins **Serves: 4-6 persons**

- Coconut milk... *400 ml*
- Eggs ... *4 no*
- Powdered sugar ...*6 tbsp*
- Dessicated Coconut ... *1 tbsp*
  Or
- Fresh Coconut grated ... *½ cup*
- Crust-less Bread slices ... *3 no*
- Water ... *3 tbsp*
- Vanilla essence ... *¼ tsp* (optional)

Preparation and Cooking

1. Put 2 tbsp sugar in a small micro-safe bowl and mix it with water and cook on micro High for 5 minutes, so that sugar turns into caramel.
2. Spread a layer of caramel on the base and sides of a medium sized round micro-safe bowl and keep it aside for the caramel to set.

3. Make fresh breadcrumbs by putting bread slices in a dry grinder.

4. Beat together eggs and sugar; pour the coconut milk over them and beat thoroughly; add desiccated or fresh coconut, fresh breadcrumbs and essence and mix once again.

5. Boil 2 cups water in a large micro-safe bowl on High for 4 minutes.

6. Gently pour the coconut-egg mixture in the bowl lined with caramel. Cover the dish with cling film and place it in the large bowl of hot water.

7. Cook on micro High for 15 minutes. Remove from oven and let the dish stand till the coconut caramel cools down.

8. Uncover the steamed pudding and cool under refrigeration for 4 to 6 hours before serving.

Serving: You may invert the pudding in a chilled plate and garnish it with Caramel sauce.

In this recipe the use of coconut milk makes it very different and nicely flavoured.

Variation: Instead of coconut milk, use Full Cream Milk in the same measure and follow the process.

Many people do not like the flavour of caramel, so they may omit it and instead add the prescribed measure of sugar to coconut-egg mixture.

8. Chocolate Sponge Roll

Micro Baking: 12 mins **Serves: 4-6 persons**

- Flour ... *6 tbsp*
- Coco powder ... *6 tbsp*
- Baking powder ... *½ tsp*
- Salt ... *¼ tsp*
- Egg whites ... *4 no*
- Sugar ... *¾ cup*
- Egg yolks ... *4 no*
- Vanilla essence ... *1 tsp*
- Powdered Sugar... *½ cup*
- Fresh Cream whipped ... *½ cup*
- Towel duster
- Baking tray ...*9"x14"x1"*

Preparation and Cooking

1. Sieve together flour, coco, baking powder and salt three times.
2. Beat egg whites stiff but not dry; gradually fold in sugar.
3. Beat egg yolks until thick and lemon coloured. Add vanilla essence to the yolks.

4. Fold egg yolks into egg white mixture.
5. Fold in flour mixture.
6. Line baking tray with greased paper and pour in the prepared batter.
7. Bake in hot oven for 12 minutes.
8. Turn out on towel dusted with powdered sugar; remove the greased paper and trim crisp ends.
9. Roll up lengthwise; wrap in towel and cool.
10. Whip cream stiff and add 1 tbsp sugar.
11. Unroll cake; spread cream over it; roll up again and sprinkle with powdered sugar.
12. Wrap in a piece of butter paper or foil and keep under refrigeration to cool.

Serving: Cut into ½-inch thick slices and serve cold.

Tip: You may fill up the cake with ice cream and then freeze for some time; cut into slices and serve with hot chocolate sauce.

Chocolate Sauce: Mix together 2 tbsp Coco powder and 4 tbsp Sugar with ¾ cup Water in a micro-safe glass bowl. Cook on micro High for 3 minutes, stirring once.

Cream Icing can also be done on the cake before serving. Beat 200 ml fresh Cream with 2 tbsp icing Sugar; add a pinch of Cream of Tartar; apply on the cake and chill it before serving.

9. Dates Pudding

Micro Cooking: 15 mins **Serves: 4-6 persons**

- Milk ... *2 cups*
- Eggs ... *2 no*
- Bread slices ... *2 no*
- Sugar ... *3 tbsp*
- Clove powder ... *a pinch*
- Cardamom powder ... *¼ tsp*
- Dates ... *10 no*
- Square shaped micro-safe dish

Preparation and Cooking

1. Wash 8 dates and soak in lukewarm water for 30 minutes; remove the stones and cut the flesh into small cubes. Wash and grate the remaining 2 dates. Keep them aside.
2. Remove the sides of the bread and cut into cubes.
3. Heat milk in Reheat mode for 2 minutes and soak bread cubes in it for 15 minutes.

4. Add sugar, cardamom and clove powders.
5. Break eggs in a blender and whisk for a while. Add milk and bread mixture and blend for a minute. Add cubed dates in it.
6. Grease the microwave dish with a little butter and transfer the liquidized contents into it.
7. Cook on Combi-1 mode for 15 minutes and serve.

Serving: Garnish the baked pudding with grated dates and serve the dessert hot or cold. Date Pudding can be served with any Indian or Continental meal.

Variation: Instead of dates and cardamom powder, add 2 tbsp Coco powder, 1 more Egg and ½ tsp Vanilla essence to the other ingredients and follow the process. You will get a nice Chocolate Pudding.

10. Fruit Medley

Micro Cooking: 5-7 mins **Serves: 4-6 persons**

- Bananas ... *4 no*
- Apples/Oranges ... *2 no*
- Black Grapes/ Pears/Dates ... *1 cup*
- Pineapple pieces...*½ cup*
- Apricots ... *10 to 15 no*
- Orange juice ... *1 cup*
- Lemon juice ... *1 tbsp*
- Sherry or Brandy ...*1 tbsp*
- Mixed Nuts toasted ... *½ cup*

Preparation and Cooking

1. Peel and cut apples and bananas into 1" pieces and sprinkle with lemon juice.
2. Peel oranges and take out segments; clean and wash grapes; slice pears; chop dates; stone the apricots.
3. Place all the fruits and dry fruits in layers in a heatproof dish.
5. Mix orange juice and brandy, sprinkle over fruits; cover with a lid; heat it on Reheat for 5 to 7 minutes.
6. Open the lid and sprinkle the nuts and serve.

Serving: Serve it hot. Just ideal for winter months.

Glossary

Commonly used terms for vegetables, fruits, herbs, grains, spices, seeds, pulses and names of a few preparations taken from various languages of India and translated in English.

Aaloo	Potatoes
Aaloo-Bukhara/Alucha	Plums
Aam/Amra	Mango
Adrak	Ginger
Ajwain	Carom seeds
Akhrot	Walnuts
Amrud	Guava
Anaar	Pomegranate
Ananas	Pineapple
Angoor	Grapes
Amchur	Mango powder
Amla	Gooseberry
Arvi/Arbi	Colocasia
Arvi ka Patta/Aadoo	Colocasia leaves
Arhar/Tuvar	Toor dal
Baingan	Brinjal/Eggplant
Badam	Almonds
Badi Ilaichi	Black Cardamoms
Baking Powder	Baking powder
Besan	Bengal Gram flour
Bhakri	Crisp Roti
Bhat	Rice steamed
Bhindi	Lady Fingers/Okra
Bhutta	Corn
Boondi	Deep-fried droplets of pulse/lentil flour

Chai	Tea
Chapati	Flat griddle-roasted wheat circlet
Chaat	Savoury snacks
Chaat Masala	Powdered spices used for chaat
Chironji	Chiroli
Chholia	Green Gram
Chhote Aaloo	Baby Potatoes
Chhote Tamatar	Cherry Tomatoes
Chhoti Ilaichi	Green Cardamoms
Chukander	Beetroot
Chutney	Spicy sauce
Dahi	Curd
Dalchini	Cinnamon sticks
Dalia	Broken wheat used for porridge
Desi Ghee	Clarified Butter
Dhania	Coriander seeds
Doodh	Milk
Frace Beans	French beans
Gajar	Carrot
Ghee	Hydrogenated fat (Dalda)
Ghenhu	Wheat
Ghiya/Lauki	Bottle Gourd
Gobhi	Cauliflower
Gosht	Mutton/Meat
Gur/Gud	Coarse brown sugar
Haldi	Turmeric
Halwa	Semi-solid sweet confection
Hara Badam	Fresh Green Almonds
Hara Chana	Green Gram
Hara Dhania	Coriander leaves
Hara Pyaj	Spring Onions
Hari Mirchi	Green Chili
Hari Gobi	Broccoli
Hari Chutney	Spicy sauce of fresh mint and coriander leaves
Heeng	Asafetida/Asafoetida
Imli	Tamarind

Imli Chutney/Sonth	Spicy sauce made of tamarind pulp
Jaiphal	Nutmeg
Javitri	Mace
Jeera	Cumin seeds
Jilebi/Jalebi	Coiled tubular fried pastry soaked in sugar syrup
Kabab/Kebab	Spit roasted pieces of Vegetables, Meats or Paneer
Kabuli Chana	Chick Peas
Kachori	Stuffed patty
Kadi Patta	Curry leaves
Kaju	Cashew nuts
Kala Namak	Rock Salt
Kala Chana	Bengal Gram
Kali Mirch (Kali Miri)	Black Pepper
Karela	Bitter Gourd
Kela	Banana
Kesar/Zaffran	Saffron
Khajur	Dates
Khaskhas	Poppy seeds
Kheema	Minced Meat
Kheer	Milk and Rice sweet dish
Khichdi	Rice and Pulse dish
Kishmish	Raisins
Khoya/Mawa	Dry condensed Milk used for making Indian sweets
Khumb	Mushrooms
Khumani/Khurmani	Apricots
Kofta	Dumplings/Meat or vegetable balls
Kulfi	A frozen confection, made of thickened Milk and set in metal cones.
Lal Mirch	Red Chili
Lassi	Buttermilk/A drink made of curd
Lavang	Cloves
Lehsun	Garlic
Litchi	Litchi fruit
Machhi	Fish

Madhu/Shahad	Honey
Makhan	Butter
Makki	Maize
Malai	Fresh Cream
Maida	Refined Flour
Mutter/Matar	Green Peas
Maash/Urad	Black Gram
Masoor dal	Lentils
Methi	Fenugreek
Methre	Fenugreek seeds
Mirch	Pepper
Moong	Whole Green Gram
Moong dal	Split Green Gram
Moong Dhuli	Split and husked Green Gram
Muli	Radish
Mungphali	Peanuts/Groundnuts
Munakka	Sultanas
Murgi	Chicken
Namak	Salt
Naan	Leavened bread baked in tandoor
Nariyal	Coconut
Nashpati	Pear
Nimbu	Lemon
Palak	Spinach
Paneer/Chhena	Cottage Cheese
Paneer ka Pani	Whey
Papad	Crisp sun-dried wafers
Papita	Papaya
Payesh	A Milk-Rice dish
Phal	Fruits
Phulka/Roti	Dry puffed flour circlet
Pilav/Pulao	Meat or Vegetables Rice dish
Pista	Pistachio nuts
Paratha	Layered Roti fried on griddle or roasted in tandoor
Pua	Sweet confection
Pudina	Mint leaves

Puri	Crisp deep fried flour circlet
Pyaaj	Onions
Rabri	Clotted cream flakes
Raie	Mustard seeds
Rajma	Kidney beans
Rasa	An extract/Juice
Rava/Suji	Semolina
Safed Makhan	White home-made butter
Saag	Leafy vegetables or a dish made of them
Sarson	Mustard
Saunf	Fennel/Aniseed
Sev	Apple
Sepreta Doodh	Toned milk
Sherbet	A cool drink made of any fruit juice or rose flower.
Sirka	Vinegar
Sukha Meva	Dry Fruits
Soya Paneer	Tofu
Tamatar	Tomato
Tamatar Pulp	Tomato Puree
Tandoor	An open clay oven
Tandoori	Any food cooked in tandoor
Tarkari	Vegetables
Tatri	Citric Acid
Tejpatta	Bay leaf
Tel	Oil or cooking oil
Til	Sesame seeds
Tulsi	Basil
Urad dal	Black Gram
Varan	A dal dish made of tuvar dal
Wadian	Sun-dried, Pulse-Vegetable lumps steamed/cooked with Dals and Vegetables
Zarda	Sweet Rice preparation

Weights and Measures

(Approximate Conversion)

All powdered Spices		
1 tsp	5 gm	
1 tbsp	15 gm or 3 tsp	
All whole Spices		
1 tsp	3 gm	
Salt and other Powders		
1 tbsp	15 gm	
¼ cup	4 tbsp	60 gm
½ cup	8 tbsp	120 gm
1 cup	16 tbsp	240 gm
Vegetables		
Coriander and Mint chopped	1 tbsp	4 gm
	1 cup	60 gm
Green Peas shelled	1 cup	160 sgm
Onion chopped	1 cup	130 gm
Potatoes cubed	1 cup	150 gm
Tomatoes chopped	1 cup	225 gm
Dals, Cereals and Grains		
All Dals and Lentils	1 cup	200 gm
All Grains	1 cup	200 gm
Rice	1 cup	200 gm
Semolina (Suji)	1 cup	200 gm

Flours		
Whole Wheat flour	1 cup	135 gm
All purpose flour (Maida)	1 cup	125 gm
Breadcrumbs	1 cup	100 gm
Gram flour	1 cup	100 gm
Sugar		
Granulated sugar	1 tbsp	14-15 gm
Sugar	1 cup	200 gm
Powdered sugar	1 tbsp	8 gm
Powdered sugar	1 cup	210 gm
Dairy Products and Liquids		
Milk	1 cup	240 ml
Cream	1 cup	240 ml
Curd	1 cup	225 gm
Hung Curd	1 cup	265 gm
Cheese grated	1 cup	115 gm
Water or Juice	1 cup	240 ml
Fats and Oils		
White butter	1 tbsp	15 gm
White butter	1 cup	225 gm
Clarified Butter/Pure Ghee	1 tbsp	15 gm
Clarified butter	1 cup	225 gm
Groundnut and Mustard oil	1 tbsp	15 gm
Groundnut and Mustard oil	1 cup	220 ml
Pastes		
Ginger and Garlic paste	1 tsp	7 to 7.5 gm
Ginger and Garlic paste	1 tbsp	25 gm
Brown Onion paste	1 cup	220 gm
Almond and Cashew paste	¼ cup	55 gm
Almond and Cashew paste	1 cup	220 gm
Coconut paste	¼ cup	65 gm
Coconut paste	1 cup	260 gm

References

Mastering Microwave Cooking by Marcia Cone, Thelma Snyder

Indian Food—A Historical Companion by Dr. K.T. Achaya

Quick and Easy Chinese Cooking by Kenneth Lo